MUNCHIES

MUNCHIES

LATE-NIGHT MEALS FROM THE WORLD'S BEST CHEFS

JJ Goode, Helen Hollyman, and the Editors of MUNCHIES

Photography by Brayden Olson
Illustrations by Justin Hager

sphere

CONTENTS

Foreword   vi   Introduction   1

CHAPTER 1 **Drinks**

DIY Fernet
SAM ANDERSON   7

Midnight Sun
ANNE MAURSETH   9

Cantaloupe Agua Fresca
JESSICA KOSLOW   10

Bitter Margarita
DANNY MINCH   11

How to Drink Vodka Like a Russian
ALEXEI ZIMIN   12

René Angélil
VANYA FILIPOVIC   14

Cajun Coquito
ABIGAIL GULLO   17

How to Drink Mezcal
ENRIQUE OLVERA   18

CHAPTER 2 **Sandwiches**

Fried Shrimp and Bacon Grilled Cheese
ALISA REYNOLDS   22

Grilled Cheese
DOMINIQUE CRENN   27

Smoked Bologna and Raclette Sandwich
ERIK ANDERSON   30

Mortadella Torpedo
BRAD SPENCE   35

Tongue Sandwich
GABRIELA CÁMARA   38

Breaded Pork Chop Sandwich
ISAAC TOUPS   41

Pork Buns
DAVID CHANG   45

Tripe Sandwich
JONATHAN BENNO   49

How to Do Caviar Right
HUGUE DUFOUR   52

Chopped Chicken Liver on Toast
APRIL BLOOMFIELD   56

Soft-Shell Crab Sliders
SHION AIKAWA   59

Fried Fish Sandwich
BRANDON JEW   62

CHAPTER 3 **Things with Tortillas**

Cheese Quesadillas
ENRIQUE OLVERA   69

Pulled Pork Tacos
ARMANDO DE LA TORRE   70

Lamb Tacos with Árbol Chile and Pine Nut Salsa
WES AVILA   74

Carne Asada Burritos
MATT ORLANDO   78

Shrimp and Chili Paste Pork Loin Tacos
KEVIN PEMOULIE   81

Dirty Al Pastor Tacos with Guacachile
ROSIO SÁNCHEZ   87

Seven-Layer Dip
CHRISTINA TOSI   90

CHAPTER 4 **Hardcore**

Deep-Fried Camembert
ANDREW MCCONNELL   94

Stuffed Jacket Potatoes
NICOLAI NØRREGAARD   98

Classic Poutine
NOAH BERNAMOFF   101

Goat Poutine with Redeye Gravy
CALLIE SPEER   104

Chicken Tikka Poutine
ARJUN MAHENDRO AND NAKUL MAHENDRO   105

Tongue Chili Nachos
JEN AGG   108

Pizza
FRANK PINELLO, ALON SHAYA, MICHAEL WHITE,
KAVITA MEELU, AND PAUL GIANNONE   111

CHAPTER 5

Noodles, Rice, and Grains

Pad Thai
LEAH COHEN   121

Chinese Drunken Noodles
JEREMIAH STONE AND FABIAN VON HAUSKE   124

Gemelli Pasta with Peas, Chicken,
and Mushrooms WYLIE DUFRESNE   129

Late-Night Carbonara
MICHAEL WHITE   131

Bacon-and-Gravy Mac and Cheese
JOAQUIN BACA   134

Fried Chicken Fried Rice
JOSHUA KULP AND CHRISTINE CIKOWSKI   137

Sake and Soy–Marinated Pork over Rice
TAIJI KUSHIMA AND SHOGO KAMISHIMA   140

Nasi Lemak
DALE TALDE   145

Sautéed Vegetables with Bulgur and
Dandelion Salsa Verde DANIEL PATTERSON   148

CHAPTER 6   **Meat and Seafood**

Tuscan Fried Chicken
ROBERT BOHR AND RYAN HARDY   155

One-Pot Sticky Chicken Wings
ANDREW ZIMMERN   158

Spicy Chicken Wings
HAN CHIANG   163

Butter-Basted Crab Legs with Garlic,
Ginger, and Chili GRANT VAN GAMEREN   166

Beer and Butter–Spiked Crab in Black Bean
Sauce PHET SCHWADER   169

Salt-and-Pepper Crab with Mapo Tofu
DANNY BOWIEN   171

Miami-Style Lobster Ceviche
MICHAEL SCHWARTZ   175

Shrimp Saganaki with Feta and Tomatoes
KONSTANTIN FILIPPOU   176

Salted Ribs with Braised Cabbage
ESBEN HOLMBOE BANG   181

Oxtail Curry with Roti
STUART BRIOZA AND NICOLE KRASINSKI   183

Lemongrass and Thai Basil Pork Pie
TIEN HO   189

Porchetta
CARLO MIRARCHI   192

Meatballs and Red Sauce
THE FRANKS   195

Côte de Bœuf
ANTHONY BOURDAIN   198

CHAPTER 7   **Dessert**

Chocolate Chip and Mint Ice Cream
Sandwiches
MICHAEL CHERNOW AND DAN HOLZMAN   205

Cardamom Rice Pudding
RAJAT PARR   206

Blackout Stout Cake
AGATHA KULAGA AND ERIN PATINKIN   209

Fernet Gingerbread with Foie Gras Torchon
MAYA ERICKSON   214

Toasted Coconut–Lemon Curd Tart
ANNA TRATTLES AND ALICE QUILLET   219

CHAPTER 8   **The Morning After**

Scrambled Eggs with Uni
JOSH GIL   225

Japanese Congee
MASARU OGASAWARA   226

An Omelet
IÑAKI AIZPITARTE   231

Giant Ham and Cheese Hot Pocket
KYLE BAILEY   234

Cinnamon-Sugar Donut Holes
with Salted Caramel MITCH ORR   239

Beef Heart Bagel Sandwiches
LEE TIERNAN   242

Scrambled Eggs and Potato Chips
JAMIE BISSONNETTE   247

Acknowledgments   248   Index   250

Foreword

MARIO BATALI

As soon as MUNCHIES started filming *Chef's Night Out*, I started watching. I had a blast seeing fellow chefs like David Chang, Andrew Carmellini, and April Bloomfield enjoying a night of great eating and drinking out on the town. Then I started getting bitter. No one has ever asked me to be on an episode of *Chef's Night Out*.

The show has a beautiful premise: you get to see not only what chefs actually like to eat late at night, at the end of a long shift, but also who they are. And just like everyone else after they've had eight or so drinks, chefs aren't as carefully measured or cohesively attached to their brand as they otherwise are. They're candid.

Sometimes what takes place on camera is silly and stupid, and sometimes it's funny and insightful. For me, there has always been a grain of something fascinating in watching. Well, maybe not every minute of it, because drunk people are often idiots.

My children, much to the chagrin of my wife, joined fraternities. New fraternity brothers have to go through an experience we will call "hazing." I call it "torture." But the idea is that by facing a physical hardship together, you'll grow closer because you have all collectively passed through this gauntlet of flames.

This mentality exists in restaurant-kitchen culture, too. There may not be actual hazing anymore (there was in the 1970s, '80s, and '90s), but there's still the camaraderie among cooks born from spending a night together on the line. All day long, you prepare for what's coming, and when it happens, you go through it together, whether or not you're actually prepared. The sign of a functional professional kitchen is that no one has to yell: you're all a collective unit, so everyone already knows what's too brown or what's not brown enough; what's overcooked and what's not cooked enough; what's too much fat or acid or salt and what's just right.

You are all bound by the desire to make sure that you're achieving greatness as a team. There's a lot of blood, sweat, emotion, and bonding that happens every day. You learn to trust someone, how to anticipate when they're going to make a mistake, and how to help them recover or bury it. You also learn how to help them move forward. At the end of every day, that trust is what you release in steam by going out on the town together: you all have some beers, some shots, and you all take a collective breath. This is the beauty that *Chef's Night Out* manages to capture.

I can't think of another job where you get to go to work every day, start with an empty chalkboard, attack each situation full-on, and at the end of the day, you leave it all on the line. You leave work knowing you won, you slayed, you kicked ass. There's no *"Oh, I should be thinking about those third quarter finance reports"* at the end of the day. You're fucking done. The eagle flies every night. Cooking allows us to have a moment of sincere satisfaction every day. When you nail that Skate Grenobloise, the sauce has emulsified just right, the skate was perfectly cooked right at the bone, and you know that someone's going to eat it and say, "This is fucking perfect." It doesn't even matter if they don't know your name. That's the best thing about being a cook.

You're always hungry two hours after you've gotten off the line, most likely after most restaurants have closed and there's nothing in your refrigerator at home. That's when your cooking is at its most primordial: you want simple dishes that say more about ingredients than technique. It might be soft-shell crab or ramp season, so you drop some in the fryer and then eat them with hot sauce. It might be a few slices of steak and a very perfectly dressed salad, because that salad is really what you're craving. You might turn up the dial on seasoning, acidity, heat and chiles, or herby brightness,

because that's what you're looking for after nine or ten beers or shots. At this point, what really makes you excited to eat is something that's going to be explosive on your tongue. It's never gonna be blanquette de veau at 3 a.m.

That's the joy of late-night meals: You know it's wrong, but it's the time in your day when you crave this food the most. At 1 a.m., most cooks will look at each other and say, "Let's get out of here and go to Chinatown or a greasy burger place." We want to go where the beverages are at the right temperature—stinging cold—and we want to eat something that comes out of the kitchen fast, and satisfies the deep desire to fill our empty stomachs. For me, it might be pad thai or perhaps a stir-fry noodle.

In this cookbook, you'll find recipes that are expressions of these moments, when some of the world's best cooks channel their toil and liberation on a plate. You'll find Anthony Bourdain's côte de boeuf, April Bloomfield's smashed chicken livers on toast, and Dominque Crenn's grilled cheese. For me, the perfect late-night snack might be a pile of shellfish—half of it raw and half of it sautéed like they do at Casa Mono—tossed in a big bowl with a little garlic, olive oil, lemon juice, and parsley. It's magic because everyone picks it up with their hands. Then again, I've never been on this show.

Introduction

EDITORS OF MUNCHIES

Chef's Night Out started, as so many things do, with David Chang. Then just another profane chef on the rise, he agreed to let our cameras follow him and a few friends on one of his typical post-shift escapades. There was double-fried Korean chicken. There was beer dispensed from a tabletop keg that looked like a lava lamp. There were shots of soju. And there was real talk. The next day, a hungover Chang opened up about why he left his job at the stately Café Boulud to open a subversive ramen joint—he realized, he admitted, that he wasn't nearly as skilled as the other cooks in Andrew Carmellini's kitchen. In other words, the Momofuku empire started because David Chang was a sub-par cook.

On a whim, our quick-witted producers decided that it would be a good idea to force Chang to stumble back to his restaurant, Momofuku Ssäm Bar, to cook something. It wasn't. At that point, he really shouldn't have been that close to fire. As he struggled to compose his famous pork buns, the legendary chef José Andrés showed up and made fun of him.

It made for killer TV, even though it was on the web and even though the rambling 12-minute video broke just about every single cooking-show convention. Dave looked sloppy. The food he made looked sloppy. The night was poorly planned. Our producers had to cobble together a narrative on the fly. It was so much fun we thought we should do it again.

That was way back in 2009. The episode became the first in our video series, then called *MUNCHIES*. As it turns out, people like seeing chefs when they're not necessarily at their best. Each one racked up hundreds of thousands of views, revealing a massive audience disaffected by the cornball state of most food television—the over-produced shows hosted by grinning actors hired to pretend to cook.

So we kept the episodes coming. Jon Shook and Vinny Dotolo of Animal in L.A. grilled meat with some friends, actors, and a then-little-known comedian named Aziz Ansari. *Top Chef*–champ Stephanie Izard convinced us that "Chick Chefs" rule and Chicago food is way more than just Alinea, salad dogs, and deep-dish pizza. Anthony Bourdain engorged himself with Presidente at The Distinguished Wakamba Cocktail Lounge before cooking up a bloody côte de bœuf. Since then, we've filmed more than 130 episodes, traveling the world to hang with incredible chefs, from Moscow, Tokyo, Copenhagen, Mexico City, and beyond—drinking and eating like there's no tomorrow. The series so perfectly embodied VICE's food coverage—uncontrived, provocative and personality-packed, meaningful and fun—that relatively early on, it shed its name, becoming *Chef's Night Out* as we launched a full-blown food website called MUNCHIES.

The series continued to pull back the curtain on some of the chefs who had been elevated to celebrities, revealing them to be brash, dumb, smart, normal, fun. The response has been insane—more than 32 million views and counting. It has become as popular with insiders as it has with outsiders looking in. Among the young cooks and chefs who define the food culture of the moment, being on the show became a sign that you'd made it. Today, whenever we interview a chef, big-time or small-potatoes, for any reason, the conversation begins with the same question from them: "Can I be on *Chef's Night Out?*"

In some ways, this book is about the crazy shit that happens when we ply our favorite chefs with booze, food, and questions, and then scour their hazy minds for late-night eats. But like the show, this cookbook offers more than just drunken tales. We quickly recognized that the show was a way to explore a vibrant culture. The drunken disquisitions and stripped-down food the chefs share with us almost always follow a few minutes of sober, if hungover, explanation of the food they cook for a living. We do this on purpose, highlighting one of the many contradictions that makes the contemporary restaurant world so fascinating—the sweating tattooed 27-year-old raging behind the swinging kitchen doors, the suits and gray temples seated in the well-appointed dining room, twirling pappardelle and nibbling rabbit saddle. Cooking has become glamorous, even though it's really toil. Food has become trendy, even though nearly every aspect of making it is actually old. The people who cook for a living aren't "The New Rock Stars." And we love them despite that—no, *because* of that.

What still strikes us as remarkable is the food that the chefs cook at the end of the night. It's tempting to think of it as "drunk food," since it's typically conjured while under the influence. But it's something much more exciting. It's what they make not when they're feeding customers but when they're feeding friends. Sure, it's stuff they decide to make for late-night indulgence, but like the food that cooks

make for family meal, it reflects the love and care and skill you'd expect from food meant to feed their restaurant family. Stripped of pomp and inspired by a particularly hungry moment, what they cook often says more about the chef than the food at their restaurants does.

We thought the recipes for those dishes deserved to be recorded, and cooked. And so the pages herein are our compilation of some of our favorite moments from this show. Some of the recipes in this book are dead-simple. Some take work that's worth the effort. They all occupy that magical range between exciting and useful, aspirational and doable. They'll serve you well whether you dispatch them alone and sozzled at the stove or feed them to friends gathered at a table during a reasonable dinner hour. As all recipes should be, they're here to guide you, not to limit you. In other words, go nuts. You might choose to slip Chang's pork belly into warm Wonder bread rather than Chinese buns or smear chicken liver pate rather than foie gras torchon on Maya Erickson's Fernet-spiked gingerbread. You even start making mash-ups, family meal style, and swapping Jen Egg's tongue chili in place of the taco beef on Christina Tosi's seven-layer dip, or vice versa.

The chapters of the book are divided into sections meant to reflect certain categories favored by the chefs and to trace a path through the most delicious night of your life, beginning with temptation and ending in resurrection. There are "Drinks" to get your night started; there are "Things with Tortillas," because your descent begins with nachos, tacos, burritos, and seven-layer dip. There is a section called "Hardcore" devoted to the point in the evening when you can't remember how many cocktails you've had and you just want everyone to know how much you love them (pizzas, nachos, poutines, and more). And of course, there's the "Morning After" for all the hangover dishes to aid the anguish that awaits.

CHAPTER 1

Drinks

SAM ANDERSON

Make Your Own Fernet

NEW YORK, NEW YORK

Watch enough *Chef's Night Out* episodes, and you'll probably be struck by a few shocking things: chefs like tacos, chefs like pizza, and chefs drink a disturbing amount of fernet. If you've ever worked in restaurants, at least those where everything seems to be house-pickled or wood-roasted, you've probably ingested a good case's worth of the hate-or-love-it liqueur, though how a spirit that clocks in somewhere between licorice and Listerine has achieved such status, no one really knows. We've heard that fernet, a variety in the amaro category of bitter Italian after-dinner drinks, gained popularity because it used to be the one bottle behind the bar you could reliably sneak swigs from without anyone noticing, because no paying customer ever ordered it. Not any more.

Now that the cool kids like it, you'd be forgiven for tasting it and wondering what is wrong with them all. That is, until the moment your opinion on fernet evolves. First, there's outrage that someone said this was good. Then there's the WTF curiosity about what's in the acrid potion. Then there's the acceptance that you paid $10 for the glass, so you might as well drink the rest. And finally, "Another fernet, please." It helps that when ingested steadily through the night, fernet seems to safeguard the belly. Rumor even has it that in San Francisco during Prohibition, fernet was legal to imbibe, because it was considered medicine, not booze.

What's in fernet varies by the brand—the most common being Fernet-Branca—and even though the actual combination of herbs and spices is a closely guarded secret, you can typically bet they include myrrh, rhubarb, chamomile, cardamom, aloe, and saffron. But we wanted our own version, so we invited Mission Chinese Food beverage director Sam Anderson to hang in our test kitchen and show us the way. His version is made using home-made bitters and is so good we thought we'd share the recipe with you. First, you make bitters, which it turns out is as simple as combining spices, herbs, and other aromatics, then giving them a three-week bath in flavorless high-proof alcohol. In glass mason jars sitting pretty on your counter, they look like little terrariums—hence the name. After that, you've got cocktail bitters for the next decade and/or the makings of your own fernet. Serve fernet on the rocks with a twist, or pretend you're Erik Anderson (page 28) and take shots like there's no tomorrow.

This recipe is inspired by the fresh herbs Sam picked from the MUNCHIES rooftop garden; feel free to swap in your favorite fresh herbs.

DIY Fernet MAKES ABOUT 3 QUARTS

1 quart Terrarium Bitters
(recipe follows)

4 cups demerara sugar

2 cups rhum agricole
(aka really good rum)

Warm all the ingredients along with 1 quart of water in a large saucepan set over medium-high heat, stirring frequently, until the sugar is dissolved. Pour into mason jars, seal, and store in the fridge until, oh, the end of time. The longer you let this sit, the better it gets.

Serve chilled as shots or on the rocks with a lemon twist.

Terrarium Bitters MAKES ABOUT 1 QUART

Zest strips from
3 oranges

Zest strips from
1 grapefruit

½ bunch fresh mint

½ bunch fresh pineapple
sage or regular sage

1 stalk lemongrass,
smashed with the back
of a heavy pan

1 bunch (about ½ cup)
fresh nasturtiums (stems,
leaves, and flowers)

1 cup Sichuan peppercorns

¼ cup cardamom pods

2 tablespoons coriander
seeds

1 orange, cut into wheels

1 bunch (about ½ cup)
edible wildflowers
(optional)

1 quart neutral grain spirit
(aka flavorless 190-proof
alcohol)

Combine everything but the booze in a 2-quart mason jar, then pour in the grain spirit. Seal the jar, shake well, and store for 3 weeks at room temperature.

After 3 weeks, strain the bitters first through cheesecloth and then again through a coffee filter. Pour into a clean 1-quart mason jar. The bitters will keep indefinitely at room temperature.

As Esben Holmboe Bang of Maaemo (page 178) rampaged viking-like through Oslo, he stopped to partake from one of his favorite bartenders, Anne Maurseth. She kept him and his fellow marauders' spirits high with this bracing, spicy tipple. In the share-and-share-alike fashion of bartender culture, she was tweaking a creation from roving barman Brian Miller, who worked at New York trailblazer Pegu Club and Death & Co and now goes about the world spreading joy and cocktails—or, in celeb bartender terms, "consulting." She was the one who thought to incorporate the warming nip of cinnamon and the complex acidity of grapefruit, all in the service of showcasing a truly special spirit: Linie aquavit. It's not just infused with an enigmatic blend of herbs and spices, and it's not just aged in sherry casks. The spirit is shipped by boat to Australia and back, crossing the equator (or in Norwegian, *linie*) twice. The conditions of traveling the high seas may or may not make a difference, but this kind of lore is part of why we love boozing so much.

Midnight Sun   SERVES 1

1½ ounces aquavit, preferably Lysholm Linie

1 ounce freshly squeezed pink grapefruit juice

½ ounce Cinnamon Syrup (recipe follows)

¼ ounce freshly squeezed lime juice

1 green cardamom pod, crushed

Grapefruit peel, for garnish

Combine all the ingredients except the grapefruit peel in a cocktail shaker filled with ice and shake vigorously until your arms hurt, 10 to 20 seconds. Pour through a fine-mesh strainer into an ice-filled rocks glass and garnish with the grapefruit peel.

Cinnamon Syrup   MAKES ABOUT 1 CUP

1 cup granulated sugar

3 cinnamon sticks

½ vanilla bean, split lengthwise

Combine the sugar, cinnamon sticks, and 1 cup water in a small saucepan. Use a knife to scrape the seeds from the vanilla bean into the saucepan and add the pod halves, too. Set it over medium-high heat and cook, stirring, until the sugar dissolves. Let sit at room temperature for at least 2 hours, then strain the syrup into an airtight container. Store it in the refrigerator for up to 3 months.

FROM LEFT: Bitter Margarita (page 11), Midnight Sun, Cantaloupe Agua Fresca (page 10)

The folding sign outside of Sqirl says "Toast and Coffee." As anyone who's stood on the endless line of pretty people on North Virgil Avenue knows, this is a slight understatement. It's like Tokyo's Sukiyabashi Jiro sticking a placard on the door that says "Fish and Rice." Even if you haven't actually ingested L.A.-phenomenon Jessica Koslow's thrilling healthy(ish) food, you've almost certainly vicariously experienced her cheffed-up brown rice bowls and unreal burnt brioche slathered with ricotta and housemade jam—#sqirl #lovinlife photos on Instagram are the latest in humblebrag technology. Don't be fooled—her menu might be heavy on the vegetables, served in hashes, salads, and lacto-fermented pickles, but neither food nor chef is abstemious. Koslow's after-hours meal took the form of a mini block party (and fundraiser, aw!). She teamed up with Mariscos Jalisco, a Boyle Heights institution-on-wheels, for shrimp tacos and tuna tostadas, and we left pining for her *agua fresca*—the magic Mexican beverage of fruit tricked out with sugar and lime. Tequila is optional but recommended.

Cantaloupe Agua Fresca   SERVES 1

Tajín seasoning, for the rim (optional)

4 ounces Cantaloupe Juice (recipe follows), plus a little extra for the rim

1 ounce any good blanco tequila

½ ounce freshly squeezed lime juice

Cantaloupe balls, for garnish (optional)

Fresh mint, for garnish (optional)

Sprinkle plenty of Tajín on a plate. Dip the rim of a collins glass into some cantaloupe juice, then invert it onto the Tajín, pressing and turning the glass so Tajín sticks to the rim. Fill the glass with ice. Pour the cantaloupe juice, tequila, and lime juice into a cocktail shaker filled with ice. Shake vigorously, then strain into the prepared collins glass. If you want to get fancy, garnish with cantaloupe balls and mint.

Cantaloupe Juice   MAKES ABOUT 6 CUPS

1 (4¼-pound) cantaloupe, peeled, seeded, and roughly chopped

5½ ounces (⅔ cup) granulated sugar

Leaves from 1 bunch fresh mint

Freshly squeezed lime juice, to taste

Put the chopped cantaloupe, sugar, and mint in a blender and puree until smooth. Add a splash of water to thin the puree to the consistency of juice, then add lime juice to taste. Strain through a fine-mesh strainer into a pitcher and use immediately or store covered in the fridge for up to 3 days.

We will never tire of new-fangled cocktails, the ever-increasing library of drinks with impish names and concocted from obscure liquors that require covert googling to ID. But ultimately, just about every cocktail is someone's riff on another, and we appreciate when bartenders get straight to the point. That's one reason we celebrate Danny Minch, the co-owner and barman at Walter Foods in Brooklyn. His take on the margarita is exactly what it sounds like—the classic guzzleable adult beverage made a wee bit cerebral with a splash of Campari subbed in for some of the Cointreau. The addition of the herbal, bitter Italian aperitif means you'll probably sip more slowly and thoughtfully before you shake up another.

Bitter Margarita SERVES 1

2 ounces any good blanco tequila

¾ ounce freshly squeezed lime juice

½ ounce Cointreau

¼ ounce Campari

Lime wedge, for garnish

Combine the tequila, lime juice, Cointreau, and Campari in a cocktail shaker filled with ice. Shake until your arms hurt, 10 to 20 seconds, then strain into an ice-filled rocks glass. Garnish with the lime wedge.

ALEXEI ZIMIN

How to Drink Vodka Like a Russian

MOSCOW, RUSSIA

All the stories you hear about Russians and vodka are true. Take Alexei Zimin, the almost-dentist turned celebrity chef. The guy studied under French legend Raymond Blanc, owns the Moscow restaurant Ragout, writes cookbooks, hosts TV shows, and runs *Eda,* the *Bon Appetit* magazine of Russian, all while maintaining a camaraderie with the bottle. Indeed, when he took us around the frozen streets of Moscow, he mainly hewed to tradition, consuming herring, beets, mayonnaise, and a troubling amount of his country's spirit of choice. It brought out the poet in him: He held up a bite of brown bread with herring and used it as a metaphor for the Russian condition: "It's the story of one fish from a can of many fishes," he said. "Left alone between two slices of hot bread. With a shot of strong alcohol, it makes you confront reality. This is the fish and also you." It sounds especially profound when you're a liter deep. Things got even hazier from there. When the camera stopped rolling, on the steps of the best cocktail bar in Moscow and while a pianist played Lennon's "Imagine" inside, Alexei's blotto friend coldcocked our field producer.

We learned so much from the illustrious chef that evening. What we will carry within us forever is the proper procedure for drinking like a Russian:

1   Order vodka by the bottle, not the shot.

2   Drink enough to encourage a certain freeness of spirit.

3   Chase each drink with a bite of pickle. Yes, the Russians basically invented the pickle back.

4   Find a comfortable stage, preferably somewhere dark and snowy.

5   Sing a melancholy song with feeling, preferably in Russian, though not necessarily on key.

Pity the fool who goes to Montreal and doesn't have dinner at Joe Beef.
Or that is, doesn't at least *try* to nab a table at the Little Burgundy restaurant to gorge on the food equivalent of a bear hug from a portly Quebecois:
heaps of horse tartare; cream-lavished, bacon-studded tangles of spaghetti
topped with the sweet flesh of entire lobsters; and a disquieting riff on KFC's
Double Down (made with foie gras instead of chicken) that would've given
Louis XVI pause. But it's not just the food that makes the place so vital.
It's the organic exuberance of its chefs, David McMillan and Fréd Morin, and
the place itself—the former crack den-turned-garden out back, the chalkboard menu on the wall scrawled with exciting French words, the occasional
untranslatable dish (along the lines of "corn flake eel nuggets"!) and funky,
old-world wines not even your geekiest friends have heard of. If you want a
taste, either book a ticket or cuddle up with some smoked meats and a copy
of their cookbook. Or shake up a René Angélil, the strong, bracing cocktail
created by beverage director Vanya Filopovic and named by the roguish
minds at Joe Beef for the late husband of fellow Quebecois superstar Céline
Dion. It's a great cocktail to fuel your evening out (or in), and emblematic of
the Joe Beef experience: French Canadian culture celebrated, for better or
worse, in full force.

René Angélil   SERVES 1

1 ounce bourbon

1 ounce Amara Amaro
D'Arancia Rossa

2 dashes Angostura bitters

Freshly squeezed juice of
half a lime

Grapefruit soda, such
as San Pellegrino
Pompelmo, for topping off

Lime wedge, for garnish

Combine the bourbon, amaro, bitters,
and lime juice in an ice-filled mixing glass,
then stir for a good 15 seconds. Strain
into a rocks glass filled with ice and top
off with a generous splash of grapefruit
soda. Garnish with the lime wedge.

The daiquiri is, and always was, a party drink. The original concoction of rum, lime, and sugar entertained profiteers on the Cuban beach from which the cocktail takes its name. The Hemingway daiquiri, which also contained maraschino liqueur and grapefruit juice, was drunk so eagerly by its name-sake Ernest that we'd venture to say its spirit, though not its formula, might have inspired the New Orleans daiquiri, a category of blended frozen cock-tail designed to get you wasted. Not that Louisiana residents needed any help getting lit. They still have drive-through daiquiri stands that dispense them in "go cups," and it's been only about a decade since you could actually drink it in moving vehicles, so long as you weren't doing the driving.

So of course, when Nina Compton, chef of Compère Lapin, in New Orleans, started her night out, she and her crew did so with go cups of the good stuff in hand. Made by the restaurant's star bartender, Abigail Gullo, this version follows the strict formula of the highly traditional Big Easy version: It's good and sweet, and spiked with myriad liquors. But hers is carefully blended, the various spirits contributing just the right level of complexity to balance all that sugar. The coconut addition is inspired by the Puerto Rican coquito cocktail, and means the drink goes as well with Compton's Caribbean-influenced cooking.

Cajun Coquito   SERVES 1

4 ounces Coquito Mix (recipe follows)

1 ounce cane syrup (like Steen's), maple syrup, or simple syrup

¾ ounce light rum, preferably Bacardi

¾ ounce spiced rum, preferably Old New Orleans

½ ounce coconut rum, preferably Rhum Clément Mahina Coco

½ ounce pimento dram, preferably Hamilton

½ ounce Licor 43

Combine all the ingredients in a blender, add 2 cups ice, and blend until smooth. Pour into large plastic cup and serve with a straw.

Coquito Mix MAKES JUST OVER 2 QUARTS

1 pint half-and-half

1 (15-ounce) can sweetened coconut cream, preferably Coco Lopez

1 (14-ounce) can sweetened condensed milk

1 (13.5-ounce) can unsweetened coconut milk

1 (12-ounce) can evaporated milk

Combine all of the ingredients in a large bowl and stir well. Transfer to mason jars and refrigerate, covered, for up to 5 days.

How to Drink Mezcal

MEXICO CITY, MEXICO

Let the record reflect that in the annals of *Chef's Night Out*, mezcal was drunk at least as often as fernet. And that's saying something. When some of the world's greatest cooks were let loose, whether they had roots in mezcal's homeland (like Enrique Olvera and Rosio Sánchez) or not (Esben Holmboe Bang in Oslo, Carlo Mirarchi in New York), they opted for the spirit often called "elixir of the gods."

No longer synonymous with cheap tequila (indeed, quite the opposite) or known just for containing a grub in the bottom of the bottle (which is not just atypical but entirely beside the point), mezcal has officially become something even lay drinkers understand should be savored like fine whiskey, not choked down like Jagermeister. Or gulped like tequila, for that matter. According to Olvera, "Mezcal is like wine from Burgundy. It has many terroirs." Mexico's most famous chef (page 66) was talking about the joy of drinking a spirit that's endlessly interesting.

While tequila is made with one type of agave (blue) and in a circumscribed region, mezcal can be made with any one of a hundred varieties, each bringing its own distinct qualities, and from many states in Mexico, which also contribute to the spirit's character. And though he's definitely no tequila hater, he admits that it's become a mostly industrial product, with the vast majority produced by giant companies. Mezcal, on the other hand, is crafted in small villages by *mezcaleros* who learned the art from grandfathers and great-grandfathers. Mezcal is agnolotti made by a Piedmontese grandma; tequila is linguine made by Barilla.

The mezcaleros bake agave in pits lined with volcanic rock and made red hot by wood fire, then crush them to a pulp using a stone wheel. Olvera has gnawed on the cooked agave left behind after the grinding. "It's incredibly complex, almost like a date mixed with pineapple and sugarcane." Once the pulp is fermented and distilled in either copper or clay, it's bottled and savored by those who know that while the spirit is made for revelry, every glass of it represents both craftsmanship and toil. It is artisanal AF. And since most of the agave varieties used for mezcal are still wild, and some take decades to mature, it'll probably stay that way.

The same qualities that make mezcal such a thrill to sip also make it a bit intimidating to order. So we asked Olvera to guide us.

DRINK IT. This is Olvera's deceptively simple wisdom, like when a yogi advises that you pay attention to your breathing. If you want to start ordering mezcal, then pull the trigger and get to know it.

INVESTIGATE DIFFERENT AGAVES. You should sample mezcales made from *espadín*, a common variety that's typically cultivated, but make sure to try those crafted from wild agaves, too—*Tepeztate*! *Barril*! *Tobala*! Olvera's fave is the innocuously named *Mexicano*, particularly when made and distilled by El Jolgorio—balanced and subtle without the polarizing qualities of bolder types. For the Scotch whisky heads, think more Talisker than Ardbeg.

ASK ABOUT ALCOHOL CONTENT. Not because you're worried about your level of blotto. But as a general rule, Olvera has noticed that the higher the alcohol content, the more you can taste the agave. In the States, mezcal usually clocks in around 45% ABV. Look for those that creep up toward 50 to 60%. He's had mezcal in Oaxaca that was 90% ABV. (You're supposed to think, *Whoa*.)

LEARN THE PRODUCERS. He looks for a few in particular, and you should, too: Koch, Cinco Sentidos, El Farolito, and El Jolgorio (which is perhaps your best bet at fine liquor stores in the States). Whatever you do, don't call them brands—after all, "Mezcal is not cologne."

DON'T DRINK MEZCAL. KISS MEZCAL. We all know you shouldn't shoot mezcal like it's Cuervo at a bachelorette party. But like many a mezcal admirer, Olvera recommends an even more restrained method of imbibing. Don't even quite sip the stuff—just let it wash over your lips. "That way you can really taste the agave. And also not get shit-faced." Let the record reflect: we can't always resist.

HOW TO DRINK MEZCAL

1. DRINK IT

2. KISS IT

CHAPTER 2

Sandwiches

When Alisa Reynolds was considering becoming a chef, she sought counsel from a friend's father. "You're too old, you're black, and you're a woman," he said. "I wouldn't do it." Needless to say, she didn't listen. Instead, she opened her own place, called My Two Cents, because while she might not be one for taking advice, she's not shy with hers.

Reynolds calls what she's going for "evolved nostalgia." So, the shrimp and grits and stuffed pork chops still taste like the indulgences you remember, but she uses her culinary prowess to lighten them up. As it should, this thoughtfulness goes out the window when she gets turnt: back at her place, she makes fried shrimp grilled cheeses and lightens them up with crispy bacon. We're giving you the recipe for one sandwich, but if you lack a sense of shame, know that the recipe quadruples nicely, as long as you use a large skillet and fry the shrimp in batches so you don't crowd the oil.

4 strips bacon

¼ cup cornmeal

1 teaspoon Cajun seasoning

3 large eggs

Canola oil, for frying

8 large shrimp, peeled and deveined, tails removed

1 tablespoon butter, softened, plus extra for fun

2 slices bread or your favorite large sandwich roll

4 slices provolone cheese

Fried Shrimp and Bacon Grilled Cheese   MAKES 1 SANDWICH

Heat a 10-inch cast-iron skillet over medium heat, add the bacon strips, and cook, turning once, until they're crisp, about 10 minutes. Transfer the bacon to paper towels, reserving the bacon fat for another use.

Position the oven rack in the center of the oven and preheat the broiler. In a medium bowl, mix the cornmeal with the Cajun seasoning. In a separate bowl, whisk the eggs. Set them both aside for the moment.

Wipe the skillet clean. Heat ½ inch of canola oil over medium-high until hot. One by one, dunk the shrimp into the beaten egg, add it to the cornmeal mixture to coat lightly, then transfer to a plate. Add the shrimp to the oil and cook until golden and crisp, 2 to 3 minutes, turning once. Transfer them to paper towels to drain.

Spread ½ tablespoon of butter on one side of each slice of bread or the top and bottom of the roll. Put the bread, buttered-side down, on a baking sheet or broiler tray, then add 2 slices of cheese to each piece. Broil until the cheese melts and the buttered sides are lightly golden, about 2 minutes, checking after 1 minute to avoid burning.

Remove from the oven and perch the golden shrimp and crispy bacon atop the melted cheese on one of the bread slices. Top with the other slice, cheese-side down.

Heat a grill pan over medium. Carefully add the sandwich and cook on both sides until golden brown and slightly charred, about 2 to 3 minutes per side. Serve immediately.

Atelier Crenn

SAN FRANCISCO, CALIFORNIA

We're totally impressed that Dominique Crenn is, at least as of this writing, the first and only female chef in the United States to be awarded two Michelin stars, and that she scored a World's Best Female Chef award—which she was both grateful for and judiciously skeptical of. The food at Atelier Crenn, her tasting-only spot in San Francisco where the menu is a literal poem, with one line per course, blows us away every time. She could spit a freestyle in French with each plate, and we'd still drop $350 a head. But we were equally impressed that she took us cheese shopping at 11 p.m. Between dinner and a final cocktail, she stepped into the now-gone and much-missed Gourmet & More (and metaphorically back to her childhood in Brittany), ogling the cheeses at this Hayes Valley épicerie and then leaving with both a haul and a purpose.

To those who work with Crenn, it was basically a given that after her wine-fueled jaunt around the city she'd make grilled cheese. It's what they make for her, without a word necessary from Chef, practically every night, when service is winding down and the boss is itching for a snack to eat with her nightly glass of rosé. The formula is butter-griddled brioche, then more butter between the bread and the grated Comté, then finally a melty trip in the oven. Sometimes they lay on a slab of ripe tomato or some trim from black truffle, if they have any hanging around the kitchen.

Since Crenn was *très* tipsy, she went a bit off script on the night we spent blessed by her presence. Instead of making grilled cheese in the French tartine style (rough translation: open-faced) that she grew up with, she executed the sort more familiar to those of us who grew up eating at diners on the NJ Turnpike. Yet these *killed* the rye-with-Kraft singles sandwiches of drunken evenings past. To recreate Crenn's, we took her "you do you" advice, while also homing in on Crenn's nonnegotiables—you can use any type of cheese, any amount of butter, and any kind of bread (brioche! sourdough!) you'd like to as long as they're all top quality.

Because we respect her dairy game, we asked Crenn how she chooses cheese for melting on bread—a question only a true grilled cheese buff takes seriously. And she did. She's a fan of mixing varieties—up to four kinds—and isn't scared of heating up the good stuff. Her first tip is to ask your cheesemonger, also known as the person behind the counter at a place that stocks more than industrial Brie and Cabot cheddar. A lactic whisperer will guide you toward the fatty cheeses that liquefy, rather than separate, when heated. For Crenn, that might be a no-brainer like Raclette or a triple crème, such as Explorateur or a stateside option like Cowgirl Creamery's Mt Tam. She's partial to Gruyère, too, which her mom used for gratins when she was a girl, although her guy at Gourmet & More turned her on to L'Etivaz. It's made by renegade former Gruyère makers who insist on using milk from cows grazing in Alpine meadows during summertime, then turn it into cheese using copper cauldrons heated over wood fires. Oozing between bread, it is indeed worthy of a poem.

When it comes time to cook, though, we still go all in on her beloved Comté, which tastes as nutty as a Trump surrogate and melts under heat like a tween at a Taylor Swift concert. And because we respect the queen, we also applied her genius butter-bread-butter technique, which won us over even when we slipped up and used our pet processed product, yellow American.

Grilled Cheese   MAKES 1 SANDWICH

Plenty of good-quality unsalted butter, softened, for spreading on the bread

2 thick slices of your favorite bread

½ cup coarsely grated cheese

Heat a cast-iron skillet over medium heat. Generously butter both sides (yeah, both!) of each slice of the bread, top evenly with the cheese, and add the other slice of bread. Cook in the skillet until the bottom is golden brown, about 4 minutes, then flip over and cook another 3 minutes, until the cheese is melted and the second side is golden brown. Transfer to a cutting board and cut the sandwich in half, then serve.

Catbird Seat

NASHVILLE, TENNESSEE

If you've ever wondered how many shots of Fernet-Branca it takes to inspire half a dozen chefs to discuss the mechanics of trussing a dead baby, just ask Erik Anderson. He and his merry frat pack of cooks downed so many fernets during a night out in Nashville that their intake is best measured in multiples of 750 ml. Anderson's consumption of the bitter Italian digestif and sundry gut bombs during his Music City expedition worried even our most grizzled producer-slash-cameraman, James. Most chefs *appear* to go hard for the cameras, but have the sense to leave at least a few plates and bottles unfinished. This guy? Not so much, hence the weird conversational turn.

When we partied with him, the former roadie turned cook had just brought tweezer food—of the delicious variety—to Nashville with Catbird Seat, a thirty-two-seat chef's counter-style restaurant he'd opened with his friend Josh Habiger. Both had put in time at the résumé builders of the day (The French Laundry and Noma for Erik; The Fat Duck and Alinea for Josh), but they seemed fully at ease eating fried things and drinking terrifying amounts of fernet chased with tall boys of Naragansett.

When they hit up Rolf and Daughters for just "a few bites," Philip Krajeck's kitchen murdered the Catbird Seat crew with food. In awe of the rate of their tippling, Krajeck wondered, "Should I just put a bottle of Fernet on the table?" Krajeck then joined them at the Nashville outpost of Sean Brock's Charleston restaurant, Husk, where chef de cuisine Morgan McGlone "crushed" them in observance of the inscrutable restaurant tradition, wherein friends of the house are served ungodly amounts of food intended not so much to please as to hurt. There were crispy pigtails, rice cakes, oysters, chicken gizzards, fried chicken doused in honey, and a 43-ounce ribeye with a side of bone marrow that the table of chefs greeted with a "Fuck you."

The fact that everyone was still standing at the end of the night after the feast at Catbird Seat makes you wonder if a steady infusion of Fernet confers some kind of protective spell over one's gut. The evening ended with fried bologna sandwiches, the apogee of "trashy Southern food" and a Nashville specialty, which Erik and his cooks gave only the mildest of high-falutin' touches—smoking the log of emulsified pork product (à la local BBQ legend Pat Martin) and topping slabs with a waterfall of "Freedom Cheese" made from Raclette and Velveeta. A parting shot of fernet was dedicated to the Catbird team, who had a rough morning ahead of them.

ERIK ANDERSON

1 (5-pound) roll bologna

1 (18-ounce) bottle spicy barbecue sauce, preferably Sweet Baby Ray's

12 sweet hamburger buns, such as King's Hawaiian

RACLETTE CHEESE SAUCE

2 cups heavy cream

8 ounces processed cheese product, such as Velveeta, cut into ½-inch cubes, at room temperature

2¼ pounds raclette cheese, rind removed, cut into ½-inch cubes, at room temperature

Kosher salt

Smoked Bologna and Raclette Sandwich MAKES 12 SANDWICHES

Following the manufacturer's instructions, set up a stovetop smoker, such as the Cameron brand, with hickory woods chips to cook at about 250°F. (If you don't have a stovetop smoker, get one.)

Score the bologna all over in a crosshatch pattern, like you would a lobe of foie gras, then cut it crosswise into 6 to 8 slabs, or as many as will fit in the stovetop smoker in a single layer. Put the bologna slabs on the smoker rack and smoke, brushing often with the barbecue sauce, until the bologna tastes awesomely smoky, about 45 minutes.

Meanwhile, make the cheese sauce: Bring the cream to a boil in a small saucepan, then pour it into a blender. With the blender running on medium speed, add the processed cheese and blend until smooth, then add the raclette and blend until smooth. Pour the mixture back into the saucepan, season with salt, and keep covered until ready to use, up to 30 minutes.

When the bologna is done smoking, let it rest like a bone-in rib eye, then cut into ½-inch-thick slices. Make sandwiches with the burger buns, the bologna, and lots of cheese sauce. Get fat.

Amis

PHILADELPHIA, PENNSYLVANIA

Brad Spence is living his best life. As a good South Jersey boy, Brad was steeped in the joys of chicken piccata, scungilli marinara, and other exemplars of the local soul food. When he grew up, lucky Brad happened to train under Marc Vetri, one of the very few gods of Italian food in the United States without an orange ponytail, and—lucky us—he convinced Vetri to let him open an easygoing spot devoted to the grub you'd find at a trattoria in the Old Country, or at least food that wouldn't seem out of place in an ambitious but unpretentious spot in Testaccio.

Brad's tastes in food run in the same vein as what he prepares—lots of flavor, zero bullshit. His taste in friends, however? Lots of bullshit, lots of Philly flavor, and the kind of ribaldry that made even us blush. Brad hit up Paesano's, which elevated the sandwich game in a sandwich town (sorry, hoagie)—without resorting to that grim staple, the cheese steak. The owner is native son Peter McAndrews, who later that night would make the birthplace of American democracy proud by comparing Brad's 15-pound homemade mortadella to a certain bovine anatomical feature, among other riffs befitting the "encased meat." Peter's challenger for the evening's "most likely to get punched in the face" trophy was Han Chiang, a chef we met over plates of tripe in chile oil and dan dan noodles at the Old City location of Han Dynasty, his expanding Sichuan restaurant empire. Han manages to insult both ignorant American customers too stupid to stir said

noodles before eating them and owners of Chinese takeout joints selling $4.50 lunch specials. (So obviously, we gave him his own episode, page 160.)

They all convene at Amis for a between-bread masterpiece that still gives our grizzled producer Chris Grosso a sandwich boner. He's haunted by visions of Spence tiling an entire scooped-out sesame loaf with *warm* mortadella—which is to sad American bologna what Spence's fresh pasta with duck ragu is to Spaghetti-Os—and topping it, in proper elevated hoagie fashion, with fresh escarole, thin slices of red onion, and handfuls of Pecorino Romano. The real killers for poor Chris were the chile-spiked mayo and the fact that Spence made the 15-pound mortadella himself, carving the emulsified sausage of pork shoulder and fat, studded with pistachios and cubes of still more fat, into warm, quivering slices. We show you how to approximate this magic moment by poaching a hunk of store-bought mortadella, then carving it yourself. But if you're not up for it, order your mortadella thinly sliced.

1 (2-pound) piece mortadella

1 very large loaf sesame bread, split horizontally

½ cup mayonnaise

¼ cup sambal oelek chili paste

½ head (about 7 ounces) escarole or iceberg lettuce, cored and shredded

1 medium red onion, thinly sliced into rings

Kosher salt and freshly ground black pepper

¼ cup extra-virgin olive oil

½ cup finely grated Pecorino Romano cheese

Chips and cold beer, for serving

Mortadella Torpedo   SERVES 8

You can totally eat the meat cold or at room temp, but come on! To heat up your mortadella, bring a large pot of water (enough to submerge the meat) to a low simmer. Add the mortadella and cook until it's heated through, 12 to 15 minutes.

Meanwhile, position an oven rack in the center of the oven and preheat the broiler. Using your hands, scoop out and discard some of sesame bread's interior and reserve it for another use, like making breadcrumbs or croutons. Toast the halves, cut sides up, under the broiler until golden brown, about 2 minutes, checking after 1 minute to prevent burning. Meanwhile, combine the

mayonnaise and sambal oelek in a bowl and stir well. Spread the sambal-mayo mixture evenly on the cut sides of the warm bread halves.

When the mortadella is nice and warm, use tongs to transfer it to a paper towel–lined plate and pat it dry. Cut the mortadella into thin slices. Layer the mortadella slices on one half of the sesame bread. Top with the escarole and then the onion. Season with salt and pepper and drizzle with the olive oil. Sprinkle with the Pecorino Romano, then close the sandwich, pressing firmly to compact the filling. Cut crosswise into eighths and serve with chips and beer.

Contramar

MEXICO CITY, MEXICO

Anyone who thinks eating in Mexico City is all street-side tacos and tasting menus at Enrique Olvera's Pujol should meet Gabriela Cámara. Contramar, one of her restaurants in Colonia Roma, epitomizes the modern, urban chill of Distrito Federal (D.F.), and it still draws the cool kids and bigwigs even after two decades in business. (Her other restaurants include the Baja cuisine–focused Meretoro, also in D.F., and the game-changing Cala in San Francisco.) Contramar gets its name from a beach in the state of Guerrero, and the food evokes what you'd eat there, with your feet sunk in white sand and your eyes on the Pacific Ocean. That means uber-fresh seafood prepared simply and thrillingly, like the *tostadas de atun* (crispy tortillas smeared with chipotle mayo and topped with pristine raw tuna) that seem to be on every table, or *pescado a la talla*, red snapper splayed, deboned, and brushed with two salsas (red on one fillet, green on the other) before it's grilled and paraded through the airy dining room.

Yet when Cámara invited what seemed like the entire city to her apartment, she homed in on what she considered perfect drinking food: something salty, crunchy, and *grasoso* (a far prettier way to say greasy). She made beef tongue, which owed its inspiration to her Italian mother and her *tacos de lengua*–loving home country, though there was no anchovy-caper-parsley sauce or fiery salsa and tortillas here. Instead, she piled *grasoso* slices (plus blood sausage for good measure) on mustard-slathered bread, then finished them with pickles, tomatoes, and melty cheese. Unless you're familiar with the cosmopolitan capital, a sandwich without a smear of beans, mayo, and pickled jalapeños might seem an odd dish for a celebrated Mexican chef. Any confusion will dissolve with a few mezcals and your first bite.

If you have any doubts about cooking tongue at home, remember that it's cheap to get, dead simple to cook, and fatty and incredibly delicious to eat. Feel free to cook and slice it a day or two ahead, but let the meat come to room temp before you make the sandwiches.

GABRIELA CÁMARA

TONGUE

1 (2¼-pound) beef tongue, cleaned by your butcher

2 tablespoons kosher salt

1 tablespoon whole black peppercorns

4 cloves garlic, smashed flat

2 bay leaves

1 fennel bulb, halved

SANDWICHES

2 tablespoons vegetable oil

1 pound blood sausage links

1½ pounds toma or fresh Asiago cheese, cut into thin slices

1 loaf rye bread, preferably sourdough rye, sliced

¾ cup whole-grain Dijon mustard

4 or 5 medium tomatoes, thinly sliced

4 kosher dill pickles, cut into ¼-inch rounds

Kosher salt and freshly ground black pepper

8 tablespoons (1 stick) unsalted butter

Tongue Sandwich SERVES 8

To prepare the tongue, combine the tongue, salt, peppercorns, garlic, bay leaves, and fennel in a large, deep saucepan or Dutch oven, then pour in enough water to cover (about 12 cups). Bring to a boil over high heat, then lower the heat to maintain a gentle simmer and cook, covered, turning the tongue occasionally with tongs, until a paring knife inserted in the thickest part of the tongue goes in and out with no resistance, 2½ to 3 hours.

Carefully transfer the tongue to a cutting board, discarding what's left in the pot. Let the tongue cool just until you can handle it comfortably, then immediately pull off and discard the outer membrane or "skin" from the tongue. (This is easy if the tongue is still hot.) Let the tongue cool completely, then slice into ¼-inch-thick slices.

Heat the oil in a large cast-iron skillet over medium until it shimmers, add the sausage links, and cook, turning occasionally, until good and hot (they're already technically cooked so you're just warming them

through), 4 to 5 minutes. Transfer the links to a cutting board, let cool slightly, then cut crosswise into ¼-inch slices. (It's ok if they fall apart.)

To make each sandwich, heat the cast-iron skillet over medium-high. Put a couple slices of cheese on a slice of bread. Holding the edges of the cheese against the bread, carefully invert it cheese-side down in the hot skillet (yep, you heard us). Cook until the cheese is melted and golden brown and crisp at the edges, about 1 minute. While the cheese side cooks, spread 1 tablespoon of the mustard on another slice of bread and top with the tomatoes, pickles, blood sausage, and tongue. Season with salt and pepper. Use a spatula to pry the cheesy bread from the skillet and flop it, cheese-side down, onto the sandwich. Add 1 tablespoon of the butter to the skillet, then cook the sandwich, flipping once, until both sides are toasty and the fillings are heated through, about 2 minutes. Eat it while it's hot.

Toups' Meatery

NEW ORLEANS, LOUISIANA

If you lived in New Orleans, life would be a hell of a lot more fun. Isaac Toups, the Cajun chef and rabble-rouser, is proof. Toups cooked for a decade under Emeril Lagasse, practicing the enthusiastic use of "BAM!" before opening Toups' Meatery, a restaurant that, like its namesake, goes all in. His food is "contemporary straight Cajun"—picture boudin balls and hog's head cheese presented on cypress planks in a rustic-modern dining room. Toups was raised on hunting and fishing in Southern Louisiana, where his family has lived for three centuries. His food is influenced as much by the crawfish boils and boucheries (communal hog butchering) of his youth as by the sauce swirls and terrines of fine dining. When you go out with Toups, there's no holding back; he's the Cajun ethos, personified: *Laissez les bon temps rouler*—let the good times roll.

We learned a lot from Toups. (1) Pregame with a flash bottle of rosé, downed quickly in big swigs straight from the bottle. (2) Start your evening at the fanciest place and work backward as you get drunker. "Everyone likes a little pat on the booty," Toups said while being pampered at Delmonico, the white-tablecloth temple of turtle soup and crab-topped veal where he spent a decade cooking for Lagasse. Recreating his old after-service shenanigans, he air-traffic-controlled everyone down the street to The Avenue Pub for dumptruck fries (potatoes + pork + bechamel = yes) and ample Wild Turkey Russell's Reserve.

This is where the real drinking began and, not coincidentally, the light roughhousing. Toups's wife, Amanda, managed to keep him fully clothed, if not in line. "Isaac, you have to cook!" she scolded as he dipped into a bag of edibles. Toups might have ended the night with "hangover" pork chop sandwiches, but it's unclear if anyone's had quite set in yet. "I'm too drunk to fry the pork chops," Toups slurred, before wrestling a sous chef into a corner. A sharp "Mommy says stop" from Amanda and a stack of golden bone-in chops stabbed through with a giant knife was enough to put an end to the mischief.

With great nights come great responsibility. You must make sure to serve your friends something that makes up for any misbehavior. These sandwiches should do it: thick, bone-in pork chops, breaded, fried, and slapped between two slices of white bread. Topped with squash pickles and some dead-simple, impressive-as-fuck espresso aioli, they'll make sure that all is forgotten, if not forgiven.

Breaded Pork Chop Sandwich   SERVES 6

4 cups buttermilk

¼ cup kosher salt

2 tablespoons jalapeño hot sauce, preferably Tabasco

1 tablespoon freshly ground black pepper

6 thick (about ¾ inch) bone-in pork loin chops

Peanut oil, for deep frying

2 cups plain dried breadcrumbs

¾ teaspoon cayenne pepper

12 slices white bread

FOR SERVING

Espresso Aioli (page 43)

Squash Pickles (page 43)

Brine the pork chops: combine the buttermilk, 2 tablespoons of the salt, the hot sauce, and 1½ teaspoons of the pepper in a 1-gallon container (a pot works well) and whisk until the salt dissolves. Add the pork chops so they're submerged, cover with plastic wrap, and refrigerate for at least 12 hours or up to 24 hours.

Drain the pork chops but don't pat dry. Pour 3 inches of oil into a large Dutch oven or a deep fryer and heat to 350°F. Meanwhile, combine the breadcrumbs and cayenne in a large bowl with the remaining 2 tablespoons salt and 1½ teaspoons pepper and stir well. One by one, add the pork chops to the breadcrumbs, turn and pat them to coat in a thin, even layer of crumbs, then transfer them to a wire rack set over a baking sheet.

Cook the pork chops two at a time in the oil, flipping them once, until they're deep golden brown and an instant-read thermometer inserted in the middle of each chop reads 155°F, 5 to 6 minutes. Using tongs, transfer the chops to paper towels to drain briefly and tent with foil to keep warm. When they're all fried, make sandwiches with the chops, bread, squash pickles, and the aioli. Serve hot, and don't forget to warn people there's a bone inside.

Squash Pickles MAKES 2 CUPS

½ pound mixed yellow and green summer squash, cut into ⅛-inch-thick rounds

½ cup plus 2 tablespoons apple cider vinegar

1½ tablespoons granulated sugar

1 teaspoon ground turmeric

½ teaspoon crushed red pepper flakes

½ teaspoon curry powder

½ teaspoon kosher salt

Put the squash in a 6-cup glass jar or other heatproof container with a tight-fitting lid. Combine the vinegar, sugar, turmeric, red pepper flakes, curry powder, salt, and 1 cup water in a small saucepan and bring to a boil, stirring occasionally. Pour the boiling brine into the jar, cover with the lid, and shake gently. Remove the lid and let the pickles cool completely, then refrigerate for at least 12 hours. The pickles will keep covered in the fridge for up to 2 weeks.

Espresso Aioli MAKES 2 CUPS

¼ cup apple cider vinegar

2 tablespoons light brown sugar

1 tablespoon instant espresso powder

1½ teaspoons Dijon mustard

2 large egg yolks

1¼ cups vegetable oil

½ teaspoon kosher salt

Combine the vinegar, sugar, espresso powder, mustard, and egg yolks in a food processor and blend until smooth. With the motor running, slowly drizzle in the oil and keep blending until the aioli is smooth and thick. Add the salt and briefly blend. Serve right away or transfer to an airtight container and keep in the fridge for up to 1 week.

Momofuku

NEW YORK, NEW YORK

The first episode of *Chef's Night Out* was an experiment gone wrong. A few VICE cameramen followed up-and-comer David Chang for an evening. He talked shit with his friends Peter Meehan, his soon-to-be *Lucky Peach* co-conspirator, and Sue Chan, former PR guru for Momofuku Enterprises. He gave us his take on eating out, one that so many of the chefs who would be featured shared and that became a sort of mantra for the show. "What I want to eat is straightforward stuff," he told us. "Somewhere where there's no bullshit, no pretense. You're just going to eat."

So while he would have been fêted like a king in most of Manhattan's high falutin' establishments, he and his team opted for a raucous second-floor walkup restaurant in Koreatown called Mad for Chicken. They ate crispy, spicy Korean-fried wings and drums. They downed

a significant volume of beer from a keg the size of a toddler. It was fun times. Then they careened back to Ssäm Bar, one of the early hits in Chang's catalogue, where he drunkenly made his signature pork buns.

As he brushed hoisin between steamed Chinese buns, he waxed poetic about his philosophy on late-night munchies: "What's your favorite thing to eat before you go to bed when you're drunk as shit? What are you gonna say? Oxtail? Fucking bone marrow? Bullshit. It's that fucking crappy-ass piece of pizza you ate." His rant encapsulated a truth and seemingly contradicted it at the same time: Because of course, he was currently filling those warm buns with neat rectangles of carefully, lovingly cooked pork belly. Sure, chefs are cool eating crap when they're blotto. But what's crap for them is often gold for the rest of us.

Around two o'clock in the morning, David Chang slurringly made the restaurant's signature dish: braised pork belly on hoisin sauce–slicked steamed buns—essentially Wonder Bread, Chinese style—the dish that launched a thousand buns. He, of course, did not create the form. Approximately a million years before there was a narrow East Village restaurant slinging bowls of ramen and plates of pork buns, there were Chinese cooks making steamed breads and filling them with meat. Chang's version mainstreamed the bun, probably due to the irresistible belly, with its strata of tender meat and creamy, luscious fat. When our producer asked him to explain how he prepares the belly, he told us that all it takes is salt, pepper, and "a couple hours of don't fucking worry about it." Still, he was kind enough to share his recipe, from the instant-classic *Momofuku* cookbook. Don't stop there, though. So many dishes in this book can be substituted for the pain-in-the-ass pork—from Isaac Toups' pork chops and pickles (page 41) to pork-free delights such as Jamie Bissonette's scrambled eggs and chips (page 247). If this seems kinda wrong, trust us; it's very right.

Pork Buns   MAKES 12 BUNS

PORK BELLY

1 (3-pound) slab skinless pork belly

¼ cup granulated sugar

¼ cup kosher salt

QUICK-PICKLED CUCUMBERS

2 Kirby or other small pickling cucumbers, cut into ⅛-inch-thick rounds

1 tablespoon granulated sugar

1 teaspoon kosher salt

BUNS

12 frozen unfilled Chinese steamed buns

¾ cup hoisin sauce

1 bunch scallions (green and white parts), thinly sliced

Sriracha, for serving

To make the pork belly, nestle it in a roasting pan or other oven-safe vessel that holds it snugly. Combine the sugar and salt in a small bowl, stir, then rub the mix all over the meat. Cover the pan with plastic wrap and refrigerate for at least 6 hours, but no longer than 24.

To make the pickled cucumbers, combine the cucumbers with the sugar and salt in a small mixing bowl and toss to coat. Let sit for 5 to 10 minutes. If the pickles are too sweet or too salty, drain them in a colander, rinse off the seasoning, and dry in a kitchen towel. Taste again and add more sugar or salt as needed. Refrigerate for up to 4 hours.

Heat the oven to 450°F. Discard any liquid that has accumulated in the container with the pork. Put the pork belly in the oven, fat side up, and cook, basting it with the rendered fat after 30 minutes, until it's an appetizing golden brown, about 1 hour.

pork buns, cont'd

Turn the oven temperature down to 250°F and cook for another 1 hour to 1 hour 15 minutes, until the pork belly is tender—it shouldn't be falling apart, but it should yield to a firm finger poke with the give of a down pillow. Remove the pan from the oven and transfer the pork belly to a plate. Decant the fat and the meat juices from the pan and reserve. Let the pork belly cool slightly.

When it's cool enough to handle, wrap the pork belly in plastic wrap or aluminum foil and put it in the fridge until it's thoroughly chilled and firm. (You can skip this step if you're pressed for time, but the only way to get nice, neat-looking slices is to thoroughly chill the belly before slicing it.) Cut the pork belly into ½-inch-thick slices that are about 2 inches long.

To assemble the sandwiches, heat the buns in a steamer on the stovetop: In a wok, bring a couple inches of water to a simmer. Put the buns in a bamboo steamer, cover, and add to the wok. Steam until the buns are soft and hot, 3 to 4 minutes. Meanwhile, warm the belly slices in a pan over medium heat, just for a minute or two, until they are jiggly soft and heated through.

Grab a bun from the steamer and flop it open on a plate. Slather the inside with 1 tablespoon hoisin sauce. Arrange 3 to 4 slices of pickles on one side of the bun and 2 or 3 slices of pork belly on the other. Scatter the pork belly and pickles with scallions, fold the bun closed, and voilà: pork bun. Fill the remaining buns in the same way. Serve with Sriracha to drizzle on top.

Lincoln Ristorante

NEW YORK, NEW YORK

Here at MUNCHIES, we all have our favorites when it comes to episodes of *Chef's Night Out*. They become favorites for many reasons—because a chef is funny as fuck, because the food he eats makes you jealous that you're not currently eating it, or because it's cool to see someone we admire in her element. But all of us cherish Jonathan Benno's for another reason: He hated every minute of it. The funniest part: We didn't ask him to be on—he asked us. It's like asking to borrow a hair shirt, then getting pissy about the irritation.

Sorry, chef, but you brought this on yourself.

The reason he got on board in the first place was that he'd heard his fellow NYC pasta don Michael White raving about the good times he'd had with us (and good they were, page 131). And we were thrilled when we got an email from Benno, the former Thomas Keller deputy and head chef at Lincoln Ristorante, a modern Italian restaurant where agnolotti (a sort of tiny Piedmontese ravioli) comes stuffed with guinea hen and foie gras and veal saltimbocca (albeit the version dreams are made of) and runs you around $50. He's a man used to being in control. So shit went bad. Fast.

We practically ruined his life-changing meal from Nick Kim and Jimmy Lau (then at Neta, now at Shuko) by asking him to talk about it

ITS ALMOST THE KIND OF MEAL, AND THE KIND OF EXPERIENCE WHERE YOU REALLY WANNA BE QUIET.

rather than leaving him to quiet contemplation. At one point he asked us to stop filming. At another, he gave our camera guy a deliberate, aggressive nudge, possibly fueled by frustration of having to be articulate about enjoyment. After five hours of being stalked by the lens, he was on the verge of tapping out. We forgave him because we're admittedly annoying; because the footage, especially the stuff on the cutting room floor, still makes us laugh; and because even at the end of that trying night, he made these tripe sandwiches.

This is a tripe sandwich for the people. Braised until tender, then breaded and fried like cutlets, the result has enough squidgy pleasure to thrill tripe's many superfans, but enough salty, perfectly greasy crunch to convince the skittish to embrace bovine stomach lining. Benno gets extra credit in our book for the mix of homemade and store-bought condiments. His lemony aioli is well worth the little bit of effort it requires. And the realization that even a chef with his skills doesn't attempt to improve on B&G hot peppers has already saved us hours of pickling. Oh, and if you're not up for tripe, go ahead and substitute eight pork or chicken cutlets and skip to the breading step.

Tripe Sandwich SERVES 8

TRIPE

2 pounds honeycomb beef tripe

8 whole black peppercorns

4 sprigs thyme

2 bay leaves

2 medium carrots, cut into large chunks

1 large yellow onion, cut into large chunks

1 stalk celery, cut into large chunks

Kosher salt

3 cups panko breadcrumbs

2 cups plain dried breadcrumbs

3 tablespoons kosher salt

1 tablespoon celery seed

1 tablespoon dried basil

1 tablespoon dried oregano

1 tablespoon dried thyme

1 tablespoon fennel pollen

1 tablespoon finely grated lemon zest

1 tablespoon garlic powder

1 teaspoon crushed red pepper flakes

Freshly ground black pepper

8 large egg whites

¾ cup cornstarch

3 cups all-purpose flour

Canola oil, for deep frying

TO ASSEMBLE

Lemon Aioli (page 51)

1 large ciabatta loaf, split horizontally

3 cups lightly packed baby arugula

Pickled Onions (page 51)

½ cup drained pickled cherry peppers, preferably B&G, seeded and finely chopped

To prepare the tripe, begin by rinsing the tripe in a bowl under running water for 10 minutes. Fill the bowl with clean water and soak the tripe in the fridge overnight.

The next day, heat the oven to 300°F. Drain the tripe and put it in a large pot. Cover with 4 inches of water, bring to a simmer, then drain. Repeat this process once more, then transfer the tripe to a large roasting pan. Pour enough water into the pan to submerge the tripe and add the peppercorns, thyme, bay leaves, carrots, onion, and celery. Season with a few generous pinches of salt, cover tightly with foil, and cook in the oven until the tripe is very tender, 4 to 5 hours.

Remove the tripe from the oven and let cool in the pan to room temperature. Line a baking sheet with plastic wrap. Lay the tripe flat on the prepared baking sheet. Top with another baking sheet and something heavy (a 10-pound barbell, heavy pot, 6-pack, etc.), and refrigerate overnight (this will help create flat, even cutlets).

The next day, cut the tripe into rough 6-inch squares. Set a wire rack on a baking sheet. In a bowl, combine both kinds of breadcrumbs with the salt, celery seed, basil, oregano,

thyme, fennel pollen, lemon zest, garlic powder, red pepper flakes, and 1½ teaspoons black pepper and set aside. In a blender, blend the egg whites and cornstarch until smooth, then pour into a second bowl. Add the flour to a third bowl and season it generously with salt and black pepper.

Toss the tripe pieces a few at a time in the flour to coat with a thin layer, then dunk them into the egg white mixture so they get a very thin coat. Immediately coat the cutlets with the breadcrumbs, pressing down to ensure the crumbs stick. Repeat with the remaining cutlets, transfer to the wire rack, and refrigerate for at least 2 hours or up to overnight.

Fill a deep fryer or large pot with 3 inches of canola oil and heat to 325°F. Layer paper towels on a plate or set up a cooling rack over a baking sheet. Fry the cutlets in batches to avoid crowding the oil, until golden brown and crisp, 2 to 3 minutes. Transfer the tripe to the paper towels to drain, immediately season with salt, and tent with foil to keep warm.

Assemble the sandwiches by spreading aioli on the cut sides of the ciabatta halves. Arrange the cutlets on the bottom half, then top with the arugula, pickled onions, and pickled peppers. Cut into 8 pieces and eat while the tripe is hot.

Lemon Aioli MAKES 1 CUP

4 heads garlic, top ½ inch cut off

¼ cup plus 4 teaspoons extra-virgin olive oil

3 large egg yolks

Finely grated zest and juice of 3 lemons

1½ cups canola oil

Kosher salt and freshly ground black pepper

Heat the oven to 300°F. Put the garlic heads on a large sheet of foil, drizzle each with 1 teaspoon olive oil, then wrap tightly in the foil. Roast until tender, about 45 minutes. Unwrap, let them cool, then squeeze the garlic cloves out of their skins and into a food processor. Add the egg yolks and lemon zest and juice, and blend until smooth. With the motor running, very slowly stream in the canola oil until the mixture is smooth and thick, then stream in the remaining ¼ cup olive oil. Season the aioli with salt and pepper, transfer to an airtight container, and refrigerate for at least 1 hour or for up to 2 weeks.

Pickled Onions MAKES 1½ CUPS

1 cup distilled white vinegar

¼ cup kosher salt

½ cup granulated sugar

2 medium red onions, thinly sliced

Bring the vinegar, salt, sugar, and 2⅓ cups water to a boil in a medium saucepan. Remove the pan from the heat, stir in the onions, and let cool to room temperature. Transfer to an airtight container and refrigerate for up to 1 week.

Before Hugue Dufour opened the world's greatest diner in Long Island City, Queens, experiencing French Canadian–style excess required a trip north of the border. You see, Dufour was raised on a farm in Quebec, then trained under Martin Picard at Montreal's temple of gluttony Au Pied de Cochon, where pig heads come with lobsters, bone marrow is piled with caviar, and the namesake dish is not just a whole pig's foot but one that's been stuffed with foie gras. His then-girlfriend now-wife, Sarah Obraitis, lived in Queens, which brought him to New York. Since then, the couple has opened a string of refreshingly odd and wonderful restaurants. First there was their barely refurbished Long Island City diner, M. Wells, which trafficked in veal brains; foie gras–crowned, dry-aged beef meatloaf; and Parmesan-blanketed Caesar salads made with smoky herring. When that closed, they opened the signless M. Wells Steakhouse nearby, where you could indulge in more baroque dishes like snails tucked inside beef marrow bones, a literal tower of pork chops, and *truite au bleu*, a dish made from trout that go rapidly from swimming in a stone trough near the kitchen to dead in a pot of vinegary court bouillon.

Dufour's food isn't as heavy on the fish eggs and foie as his old boss's. Yet he was one of many chefs who decided to cap their night by popping open a huge tin of that good-good. As he explained, it doesn't make sense to have a little spoonful of caviar. It's excess, after all, and should be enjoyed by the mouthful. Here's how he goes large:

1   Get some good, soft bread like sliced brioche or split English muffins and toast lightly.

How to Do Caviar Right

QUEENS, NEW YORK

2   Get a block (not a stick) of high-quality, unsalted cultured butter and cut it, straight from the fridge, into ¼-inch-thick slabs that nearly cover the surface of the bread.

3   Get a lemon for last-minute squeezing—just enough juice to provide a little balance to all the glorious fat and salt.

4   Get caviar, the type and amount depending on how much you've got available in your checking account. If you're feeling flush, in spirit and/or cash, Dufour's choice is wild sturgeon—osetra or sevruga, as long as it's legal to purchase and costs more by the ounce than a flight to Moscow. He recommends 50 grams per sandwich. He also knows that's crazy. If you dig tiny black pearls but not splurging, look to the much less pricey and (let's be serious) almost as good roe from farmed sturgeon and paddlefish, or one of Dufour's pet products, pressed caviar, a collection of broken eggs gently compacted until it's especially concentrated in flavor and downright sliceable.

5   If you're into the pink color and juicy pop of salmon or trout roe, go nuts and buy twice as much at half the price of caviar.

The Spotted Pig

NEW YORK, NEW YORK

Before April Bloomfield took over the world, she was just a Brummie with a good CV and a thing for pig's ears. Shipped in from England to helm a low-key corner restaurant in New York's West Village neighborhood, this River Café alum created the Spotted Pig (maybe you've heard of it) and helped usher in a new era of dining in New York. Going out for killer food no longer meant postponing your annual contribution to your IRA or tolerating a table of I-bankers on their third bottle of Premier Cru. It no longer even meant having dinner. Instead, you could perch ridiculously on tiny stools or, if you were lucky or a VIP, lounge in booths while snacking on featherweight gnudi drenched in brown butter and knocking back old-fashioneds at 1:30 a.m. within earshot of Jay-Z.

The Spotted Pig was practically designed for *Chef's Night Out*. In fact, even a dozen years in, the place still hosts informal, unrecorded versions of the show nightly, when cooks from the city's various hot spots wipe down their stations and converge on West 11th Street for Roquefort-topped burgers, smoked haddock chowder, and pints of cask beer. If you're patient or connected, you'll score a table.

If you're wise, you'll make sure that table fields several plates of Bloomfield's chicken liver toasts.

Like so much of what April cooks, they're essentially simple. The magic is in the details. There's the well-browned exteriors of the livers, encasing slightly pink insides, just the thing for maximizing flavor and smooshability. There's the careful smooshing; so some is creamy, and some is still chunky. There's the finely tuned balance between the sugar of port, not to mention the more subtle sweetness of sautéed garlic and shallots, balanced by the acidity of madeira. If you skimp on the bread quality, if you don't toast it so it's still soft in the middle, if you don't hit the slices with a generous slug of olive oil, lord help you.

¼ cup extra-virgin olive oil, plus more for drizzling

Heaping ¼ cup finely chopped shallots (about 2 medium shallots)

1 large garlic clove, thinly sliced

2 tablespoons dry madeira

2 tablespoons ruby port

8 ounces chicken livers, trimmed, separated into lobes, and patted dry

Sea salt flakes (preferably Maldon) and freshly ground black pepper

Small handful of small, delicate flat-leaf parsley sprigs

4 thick slices crusty bread, cut in half

Chopped Chicken Liver on Toast — MAKES 4 TOASTS

Heat 2 tablespoons of the olive oil in a large skillet over high. When it's hot, turn the heat down to medium and add the shallots and garlic. Cook until they're golden brown, about a minute. Add the madeira and port to the pan and give it a good shake, then scrape the mixture into a small bowl and set aside.

Rinse the pan and wipe it out well, then set it over high heat and add 1 tablespoon of the remaining olive oil. When the oil just begins to smoke, add the chicken livers to the pan. Cook until the undersides are golden brown, 1½ minutes or so. Carefully turn over the livers, sprinkle with salt, and give the pan a little shake. Continue to cook the livers just until they feel bouncy, like little balloons, about 30 seconds more. You want them slightly pink inside, not rare.

Turn off the heat and add the shallot mixture, liquid and all, to the pan. Shake the pan, stirring and scraping it with a spoon to loosen the crispy brown bits on the bottom, then scrape the contents of the pan into a bowl. Let it all cool for a few minutes.

Drizzle the remaining 1 tablespoon olive oil over the liver mixture and sprinkle in about 1 teaspoon of salt flakes and a couple of twists of black pepper. Use a large spoon to chop, stir, and mash the livers until some of the mash is creamy and some is still a little chunky. Coarsely chop the parsley, add it to the liver mixture, and give it all a good stir. Let it cool to room temperature.

Toast or grill the bread until crispy but still a bit soft in the middle. Drizzle the toasts with a little olive oil, spread on a generous amount of the liver mixture, and serve immediately.

When you see a line of hungry people in Austin, the chances are 99 to 1 that they're waiting on smoked, fat-riddled meat. That is, until three buddies opened the best little ramen shop in Texas. Before the Tokyo-born, Texas-raised brothers Shion and Tatsu Aikawa and Tako Matsumoto opened Ramen Tatsu-ya in 2012, the city was a barren, noodle-less wasteland, with tumbleweeds of instant ramen rolling down Sixth Street. Soon after their opening, the entire city was lining up for bowls of tonkotsu ramen.

After shots of "Bernet" (half Bulleit, half Fernet—duh) at Shangri-La, a dive bar on the East Side, the crew headed back to the kitchen at Tatsu-ya to make *tsukemen*, a ramen variation in which bare noodles come with a concentrated broth for dipping. This they spiked with Texas-style smoked brisket, an idea so good it practically spawned their newest place, Kemuri Tatsu-ya, an *izakaya* where brisket shares bowls with ramen and fish heads get chicken fried. We bugged them for the recipe for their ridiculously good soft-shell crab sliders, which don't require simmering pork bones for twenty-eight days. Round up soft-shell crabs, the humans-outsmart-nature treat that happens from spring until summer; Kewpie mayo, Japan's MSG-fueled version of Hellman's; and squishy, sweet King's Hawaiian Rolls; and it's hard to screw up this party snack.

¼ cup chili garlic sauce	2 tablespoons mirin	Vegetable oil, for deep frying	2 tablespoons Kewpie mayonnaise
Freshly squeezed juice of 1 lime	½ bunch fresh cilantro, finely chopped	1 cup cornstarch	12 sweet slider rolls, such as King's Hawaiian
1 tablespoon yuzu juice, or lemon or more lime juice	6 jumbo soft-shell crabs, cleaned (ask your fishmonger)	2 cups thinly sliced green cabbage	

Soft-Shell Crab Sliders   SERVES 6

Combine the chili garlic sauce, lime juice, yuzu juice, mirin, and cilantro in a large bowl.

Rinse the crabs, add them to the bowl, and toss to coat well. Cover and refrigerate for at least 4 hours and up to 12 hours.

Heat 1 inch of vegetable oil in a deep fryer or heavy skillet to 325°F. Drain the crabs and, one by one, toss them in the cornstarch to coat with a thin layer. Fry, in batches if necessary to avoid crowding the oil, until

golden and crispy, about 5 minutes. Transfer the crabs to a paper towel–lined baking sheet. Let cool slightly, then cut each crab in half crosswise.

In a large bowl, mix together the cabbage and mayo.

To assemble each sandwich, split a Hawaiian roll and stuff it with half a crab and a good spoonful of cabbage slaw. Eat.

Mister Jiu's

SAN FRANCISCO, CALIFORNIA

Brandon Jew holds a special place in *Chef's Night Out* history. He is the only chef to have two dedicated episodes. They trace the familiar arc of a talented chef finding his voice. After a cameo on Mission Chinese impresario Danny Bowien's episode, where he fed Bowien headcheese (okay, more like snout cheese), we learned that he was the one who got Bowien started on Chinese food in the first place. We joined Jew for Night Out #1, when he was the chef at San Francisco's Bar Agricole, but we knew we had to reprise it once he opened his own place. Because while his food at Bar Agricole showcased his Bay Area–Italian training, Mister Jiu's is so much more—the realization of identity, a reclaiming of his heritage (his immigrant father's last name, Jiu, was changed upon arrival), and an audacious attempt to redefine what Chinese-American food can be. It's food authentic to nothing and no one but himself, a Chinese American raised in San Francisco.

So when his friends had all gathered in the dining room, he didn't whip up the killer sourdough scallion pancakes or *wagyu* fried rice with bottarga with which he has won over the city. Instead, he riffed on a dish that reminded him of his grandparents—and their meals together at Micky D's. His creation was just faithful enough to the Filet-O-Fish, in that it included a bun and fish. The rest was Jew-level cooking—a beer batter that fries up to an airy crunch; a simple, perfectly calibrated slaw; and a tangy, seaweed-spiked tartar sauce that would make an actual Filet-O-Fish worth eating.

BRANDON JEW

Peanut or vegetable oil, for deep frying

1⅓ cups all-purpose flour

1 teaspoon baking soda

1 large egg

1 cup lager, preferably Anchor California Lager

1 pound skinless black cod or halibut fillets, cut into 6 pieces total

2 cups very thinly sliced green cabbage

¼ cup olive oil

2 tablespoons champagne vinegar

2 tablespoons finely chopped chervil (optional)

Kosher salt and freshly ground black pepper

Seaweed Tartar Sauce (recipe follows)

6 brioche buns, split and lightly toasted

Fried Fish Sandwich   SERVES 6

Pour 3 inches of peanut oil into a deep fryer or Dutch oven and heat to 350°F. Meanwhile, in a bowl, whisk together the flour and baking soda. Add the egg and pour in the lager, whisking constantly, until the batter is smooth. One by one, dip the fish pieces in the beer batter, letting the excess drip back into the bowl, then slip them into the oil and deep fry until crunchy, golden brown, and fully cooked, about 5 minutes.

In a medium bowl, toss the cabbage with the olive oil, vinegar, and chervil and season with salt and pepper.

Place a piece of fish on each bun bottom, slather with seaweed tartar sauce, pile on some slaw, and then close with the top bun. Eat right away.

Seaweed Tartar Sauce   MAKES ABOUT 1 CUP

2 tablespoons finely chopped shallot

1 tablespoon red wine vinegar

1 cup mayonnaise, preferably homemade

2 tablespoons finely minced fresh seaweed (or rehydrated dried), such as wakame, rinsed

1 tablespoon thinly sliced chives

Finely grated zest of 1 lemon

1 teaspoon freshly squeezed lemon juice

½ teaspoon Dijon mustard

2 garlic cloves, minced and mashed to a paste with a pinch of salt

Kosher salt and freshly ground black pepper

Combine the shallots and vinegar in a small bowl and let stand for 5 minutes to allow them to pickle a bit. Stir in the mayonnaise, seaweed, chives, lemon zest and juice, mustard, and garlic. Season with salt and pepper. The sauce will keep in the fridge for up to 3 days.

CHAPTER 3

Things with Tortillas

Pujol

MEXICO CITY, MEXICO

Enrique Olvera is dancing, eyes closed and by himself, in his restaurant's dining room. The chef of Pujol, in the ritzy Polanco neighborhood of Mexico City, Olvera has recently become a certified culinary god. Now he has achieved face-of-Mexican-cuisine status, runs a couple of restaurants in Manhattan, and boasts a seemingly permanent spot on that suddenly-a-thing list of the world's best restaurants. But his trailblazing restaurant has been open for more than fifteen years, and Olvera has been a fearless practitioner of creative Mexican cooking from day one. He still blows minds by fusing the modern and the traditional during long, multicourse meals full of caviar and ants, soft-shell crabs and fish-skin chicharrón, and various moles and salsas you've never heard of but will forever dream about.

But after drinking all the mezcal, his solo dance number, and an impromptu conga line, the man who's currently the most famous Mexican chef on Earth stumbles into his gleaming kitchen and demonstrates how *not* to make quesadillas. His buddy, arm draped over Olvera's shoulder, complains, "I'm at the best fucking restaurant in this country, and they won't feed me." So to the stove they go. Olvera digs out stale tortillas from the kitchen fridge and heats them on a griddle with cheese, folding over the tortillas with a sharp chef's knife with the dexterity of a bear wearing oven mitts. We don't need that recipe, thanks. When he sobered up, he shared one that steps up the quesadilla game, just ever so slightly.

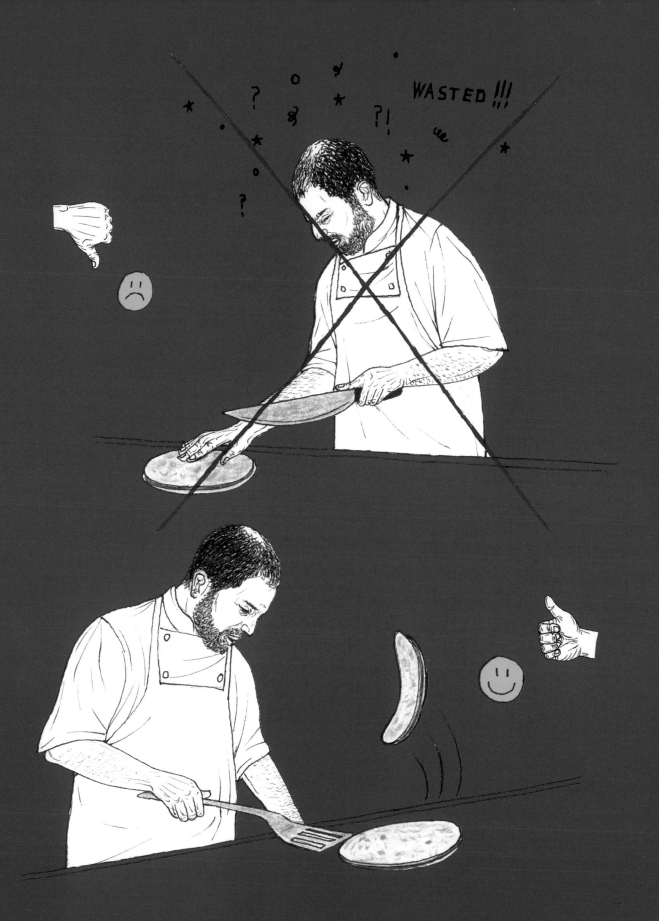

When you're in Mexico, good quesadillas—or *kekas* in Mexico City parlance—are fashioned not from premade tortillas but from fresh masa—dried corn transformed via slaked lime into dough that was nutritious enough to sustain the Aztecs and delicious enough to persist for millennia. If you buy Olvera's cookbook, *Mexico from the Inside Out*, you actually make this dough at home! The less ambitious among you will opt for fresh masa purchased from a market that sells it, which we'll admit is far easier on the West Coast than on the East. The purely practical among you will use regular old tortillas, and you know what? With some melty queso de Oaxaca, slivers of jalapeño, and an herb sprig, you'll have raised your kekas game without really trying.

Cheese Quesadillas   MAKES ABOUT 16 QUESADILLAS

16 (6-inch) corn tortillas

3½ to 4 cups shredded Oaxaca or Monterey Jack cheese

48 thin slices fresh jalapeño (about 4 jalapeños)

16 fresh epazote leaves or small fresh cilantro sprigs

Heat a large cast-iron skillet over medium-high. Add as many tortillas to the skillet as will comfortably fit in a single layer. Sprinkle 2 heaping tablespoons of cheese on each tortilla and cook until the cheese begins to melt, about 2 minutes. Add 3 jalapeño slices and 1 epazote leaf to each one, then fold the tortilla in half over the fillings. Continue to cook, flipping once, until the cheese is fully melted and the tortilla is golden brown and crisp at the edges, about 1 minute more. Eat right away.

You think you know tacos, but you have no idea. At Guisados, the father-son team of Armando De La Torre Sr. and Jr. specialize in just one of many unsung stuff-on-tortilla genres, *tacos de guisado*: stews, braises, and other delights cooked in pots rather than over a griddle before being spooned onto tortillas. The Torres opened their first location in 2010 in Boyle Heights—the area squished between Downtown and East L.A.—and on their *Chef's Night Out*, we captured some quality father-son time as each Armando showed the other his generation's Boyle Heights. For Junior, that meant creative-Italian appetizing at Bestia (technically in the "Arts District") and something called a "bone luge," where a sommelier pours sherry down your gullet via a recently scraped cow femur. For Senior, it was worshipping at the temple of Mexican-American comfort food, El Tepeyac, where two friends helped them polish off a five-pound burrito.

The drunk stomach wants what it wants. For Los Armandos, that was pork. Back in their kitchen, Armando Senior shredded some tender shoulder for Armando Junior to do the honors, aka the dirty work: toss it around on a hot griddle with the holy trinity of tomatoes, onions, and jalapeños, then pile it on warm tortillas.

2 pounds boneless pork shoulder	4 tomatoes, cored and diced	1 or 2 jalapeños, stemmed and finely chopped	**FOR SERVING**
Kosher salt and freshly ground black pepper	2 medium yellow onions, diced	2 tablespoons garlic salt	Corn tortillas, warmed
3 tablespoons vegetable oil, plus more if needed		1 tablespoon onion powder	Your favorite salsa
			Chopped fresh cilantro

Pulled Pork Tacos   SERVES 6 TO 8

Heat the oven to 300°F. Generously season the pork shoulder all over with salt and pepper and put it in a large baking dish. Cover tightly with aluminum foil and roast until very tender, about 3 hours. Using two forks, shred the meat.

Heat the oil in a large skillet over medium-high until it shimmers. Add the shredded pork and cook, stirring occassionally, until browned, about 7 minutes. Using a slotted spoon, transfer the pork to a bowl, leaving the oil behind.

Add the tomatoes and onions (and a little more oil, if necessary) to the skillet and cook, stirring occassionally, until soft, about 5 minutes. Add the pork back to the skillet, then add the jalapeños, garlic salt, and onion powder and cook for 5 to 7 minutes more. Season with salt and pepper to taste. Serve with the tortillas, salsa, and cilantro.

Guerrilla Tacos

LOS ANGELES, CALIFORNIA

L.A. did not need another taco truck. So when we got word of Guerrilla Tacos, a roving operation serving fanciful, farmers' market–inspired stuff-on-tortillas to long lines of gringos in Silver Lake, Beverly Hills, and Venice, we queued up and prepared to give it a serious eye roll. Then we tasted his masterpiece—a sweet potato taco. It had all the hallmarks of poser food. There was the sweet potato, there was butter and leeks and feta. But here's the thing: It was mind-bendingly good, anchored by a complexly spicy salsa made from almonds, chile de árbol, and tomatillos, among other things, and calibrated with sweetness, salt, and acid like all of the best dishes, fancy and not.

We knew right away it wasn't thrown together by some amateur vegetarian. The man doing the careful construction was Wes Avila. A former forklift operator and teamster turned certified fancy chef, he decided to merge his Mexican heritage and his culinary training. He traded the kitchen brigade for a no-permit, no-fucks-given taco-hawking operation (a couple of card tables set up outside a coffee shop). It became a truck, and after several years of much-deserved love from a city with high taco standards, that truck gave way to a full-on brick and mortar restaurant. This guy is an artist, and his canvas just happens to be the tortilla.

As you might imagine, the chef who convinced al pastor fanatics to embrace tacos with scallops and cauliflower loves a challenge. So he took us to Republique (the "temple of food that's fuckin' awesome"), where his old boss Walter Manzke crushed him with cocktails before sending him off with a "roadie"—a magnum of red wine and stemmed glasses. He wasn't fazed by the time he got to his happy place and the oldest tiki bar in the city: Tonga Hut in North Hollywood. Avila donned the fez he had earned by trying all seventy-two of their cocktails. As if cooking in such a state wasn't enough, he decided to tie one hand behind his back, rustling up late-night tacos at his friend Katsuji Tanabe's restaurant Mexikosher, where a rabbi was in attendance to make sure Avila didn't use pork or cheese. Avila didn't flinch, whipping up lamb tacos with pine nut salsa while guzzling Tecate—which yes, Rabbi, is kosher.

WES AVILA

1 tablespoon vegetable oil

1 pound ground lamb

1 tablespoon garlic powder

1 tablespoon onion powder

1½ teaspoons ground cumin

3 dried pequín chiles, stemmed, finely chopped

Kosher salt and freshly ground black pepper

4 tablespoons unsalted butter

8 corn tortillas

Salsa (recipe follows)

Thinly sliced chives, for garnish

Lamb Tacos with Árbol Chile and Pine Nut Salsa MAKES 8

Heat the oil in a large cast-iron skillet over medium. Add the lamb and cook, breaking it up with a wooden spoon, until browned, about 7 minutes. Add the garlic powder, onion powder, cumin, and chiles and season with salt and pepper. Cook until fragrant, about 2 minutes more.

In a separate skillet, melt the butter over medium-high heat. One by one, add the tortillas and cook, flipping once, until hot, 1 to 2 minutes. Using a slotted spoon, spoon some meat into each tortilla, then some salsa, and garnish with minced chives. Eat right away.

Salsa MAKES ABOUT 3 CUPS

1 tablespoon lard or canola oil

1 cup dried chiles de árbol, stemmed

6 garlic cloves

1 pound tomatillos, husked, rinsed, and quartered

4 ounces roasted red bell peppers (about 4)

3 tablespoons pine nuts

Kosher salt

3 tablespoons olive oil

1 habanero chile, stemmed

Red wine vinegar, to taste

Heat the lard in a large cast-iron skillet over medium-low until it melts and shimmers. Add the dried chiles and cook, stirring and flipping occasionally, until browned all over and toasty smelling, about 5 minutes. Add the garlic and cook, stirring, until the cloves are golden brown, about 5 minutes more. Add the tomatillos, bell peppers, and pine nuts to the pan, and enough water (about 2 cups) for the veggies to steam and cook. Add some salt. Bring to a simmer and cook until the tomatillos are very tender, about 20 minutes—they should split easily and break apart when pressed with a spoon. Take the pan off the heat and transfer all the ingredients to a blender along with the olive oil. Add half the habanero—or if you dare, the whole thing. Blend until the salsa is nice and smooth. Season to taste with salt and red wine vinegar; you want a little acidity, but you still want to taste some of the sweetness of the roasted peppers. The salsa will keep in an airtight container in the refrigerator for up to 5 days.

Amass

COPENHAGEN, DENMARK

Why a cook from California, home to some of the best produce in the world, ended up in a cold, dark country where potatoes and pickles count for vegetables is one thing, but how he's managed to stay is another. After two years as the executive chef at Noma—if you haven't heard of it, let us know how you like that rock you've been living under—he doubled down on the gospel of ingredient worship at his own Copenhagen spot, Amass. Even in the hellscape that is a Scandinavian winter, Orlando manages to keep 95 percent of his ingredients local, from the precious and foraged elderflower and ramson to the unsung and straight-up ugly bits, like coffee grounds to fish bones. Orlando lives for the thrill of the race—against time and scarcity and schedule—and excels at the time-honored culinary tradition of turning trash into luxury.

For Orlando, who grew up five thousand miles away in flip flops, his Noma kitchen crew became family as well as gallivanting buddies. Over at Bror in the Latin Quarter, former charges Samuel Nutter and Victor Wagman brought him whipped lamb's brains and eyeballs stuffed with mushrooms. At Manfreds, which is indeed the world's only veggie-focused restaurant famous for its raw meat,

Noma grad Christian Puglisi served his famous steak tartare. After many more beers and some unidentified shots, Orlando headed back to Amass for a little reverse cultural exchange.

The nightly after-service bonfire was raging as Orlando, like the good Cali transplant that he is, brought out the fixings for massive carne asada burritos, including the on-the-spot invention "Nordic sour cream" (drained yogurt, crème fraîche, and a slosh of the very beer he was drinking) and guacamole, which is tough to screw up even when you're hammered. And finally, because in America the only reason to have a bonfire is to burn marshmallows, he made slack-jawed wonderers of his Danish compatriots by introducing one of our greatest culinary traditions: the s'more.

HOW TO MAKE A BURRITO
HEAT
1.
2.
3. BONUS MOVE!!! FRENCH FRIES!
WRAP TIGHT IN FOIL
4.
1. COLD TORTILLA
2.
3. RICE
4.
STAY CLASSY

MATT ORLANDO

⅔ cup freshly squeezed lime juice

3 tablespoons kosher salt

4 jalapeños, thinly sliced

3 (12-ounce) Mexican-style lager beers, such as Corona or Pacifico

2 medium white onions, thinly sliced

1 bunch cilantro, coarsely chopped

3 pounds flank steak

FOR SERVING

10 to 12 (12-inch) flour tortillas, warmed

Salsa Fresca (recipe follows)

Sour cream or crème fraîche

Guacamole (recipe follows)

Carne Asada Burritos MAKES 10 TO 12

Combine the lime juice, salt, jalapeños, beer, onions, and cilantro in a bowl and whisk until the salt is dissolved. Add the steak, cover, and refrigerate for 12 hours or overnight.

Remove the meat from the marinade and pat dry with paper towels. Set up a charcoal grill to cook with high heat. Grill the steak until it's well browned on both sides and cooked how you like it, 3 to 4 minutes per side for

medium. Transfer the meat to a cutting board and let rest for 15 minutes.

Meanwhile, one by one, heat the tortillas in a large hot skillet, flipping once, until warmed through, about 5 seconds per side. As they're done, stack and wrap the tortillas in a kitchen towel. Slice the meat thinly across the grain. Season with more salt if you like. Serve the steak with the salsa fresca, sour cream, and guacamole, all wrapped up in the tortillas.

Salsa Fresca MAKES ABOUT 3 CUPS

1¾ pounds tomatoes, cored and diced

1 medium red onion, finely diced

1 jalapeño, finely chopped

½ bunch cilantro, roughly chopped

Freshly squeezed juice of 2 limes, plus more as needed

Kosher salt

In a bowl, combine the tomatoes, onion, jalapeño, cilantro, and lime juice. Stir well and season to taste with salt and more lime juice. Cover and refrigerate for 30 minutes before serving, or up to 3 days.

Guacamole MAKES ABOUT 3 CUPS

4 ripe avocados

¼ cup freshly squeezed lime juice

¼ bunch of cilantro, roughly chopped

Kosher salt

Halve and pit the avocados, then scoop the flesh into a bowl. Add the lime juice and cilantro and mash roughly with a fork. Generously season with salt, cover, and refrigerate until ready to serve, or for up to 1 day.

KEVIN PEMOULIE

Mean Sandwich

SEATTLE, WASHINGTON

Once upon a time, all the hot young things were graduating from the kitchens of Thomas Keller and Daniel Boulud. But now the students have become the masters, and their restaurants are the new incubators. Perhaps the most productive of these on the East Coast has been the Momofuku empire, which churned out what seems like half the chefs with cool restaurants in New York. Take husband-and-wife team Kevin and Alex Pemoulie, who met while working for Chang—she in the office and he as Noodle Bar's first chef de cuisine. When they were ready to break out on their own, they weren't afraid to go out on a limb, or through the Holland Tunnel for that matter. We caught them while they were running Jersey City's best restaurant, the thirty-two-seat tasting-menu joint Thirty Acres, and embracing everything that came along with Kevin's home state, from the local kitchen talent to a healthy grudge against Hoboken.

But what they cooked at the end of their evening—for, among others, Danny Bowien of Mission Chinese Food, and as a chaser for the "Italian cheeseburger" (two burger patties, ketchup, and mayo, and fries on a hero) from Jersey City institution Hollywood Fried Chicken—seems like something that would appear today on their menu at Mean Sandwich, in Seattle, where they decamped post-kid. They took pork loin, marinated it in a makes-everything-better concoction of dried shrimp, chile, and garlic, and browned it on the flattop. That night they serve it as tacos, but it's easily as delicious between bread slices or on top of a slice of pizza.

PORK AND BRINE

¼ cup kosher salt

¼ cup granulated sugar

1 (2½- to 3-pound) boneless pork loin (ask your butcher to leave a thick layer of fat on top)

SHRIMP CHILI PASTE

1 cup canola oil

3 medium shallots, thinly sliced

4 garlic cloves, finely chopped

⅓ cup (about 1¼ ounces) extra-large dried shrimp

⅓ cup kochukaru (Korean red pepper flakes)

2 teaspoons soy sauce

2 teaspoons fish sauce

2 teaspoons dark brown sugar

2 teaspoons sambal oelek

¼ teaspoon crushed red pepper flakes

PICKLED SCALLIONS

1 bunch scallions, trimmed and halved crosswise

1 cup white wine vinegar

½ cup granulated sugar

1 teaspoon kosher salt

FOR SERVING

Corn tortillas

Toasted sesame seeds

Shrimp and Chili Paste Pork Loin Tacos · SERVES 6 TO 8

To brine the pork loin, combine the salt, sugar, and 4 cups lukewarm water in a 1-gallon container and stir until the salt and sugar dissolve. Add 4 cups ice cubes and stir until melted. Add the pork to the brine, cover, and refrigerate for at least 3 hours and up to 24 hours.

While the pork brines, make the shrimp chili paste: combine the oil and shallots in a small saucepan and set it over medium-high heat. Cook until the shallots begin to sizzle, then keep at it, stirring often, until they're golden brown, about 5 minutes. Pour through a fine sieve into a large heatproof bowl. Transfer the shallots to a food processor and return the oil to the saucepan. Add the garlic to the oil, return the pan to medium-high heat, and cook, stirring constantly to keep the garlic from sticking to the bottom of the pan, until the garlic is golden brown, about 5 minutes. Pour through the fine sieve back into the bowl, transfer the garlic to the food processor, and return the oil to the saucepan; set the pan aside.

Add the dried shrimp to the food processor and process until the mixture is finely ground. Transfer the mixture to the saucepan along with the kochukaru and set the pan over medium-high heat. Cook the paste, stirring often, until it soaks up most of the oil and the unabsorbed oil is brick red, about 3 minutes. Stir in the soy sauce, fish sauce, brown sugar, sambal oelek, and red pepper flakes and cook, stirring, to meld the flavors, about 2 minutes. Transfer the paste to a bowl and let cool completely.

Remove the pork from the brine, rinse, and dry thoroughly; discard the brine. Cut the pork into 2-inch chunks, then transfer to a large resealable plastic bag. Add the shrimp chili paste to the pork, seal the bag, then massage the pork through the bag until it is evenly coated. Refrigerate for at least 12 hours or up to 3 days (the longer the better).

To make the pickled scallions, put the scallions in a medium heatproof bowl or jar. In a small saucepan, combine the vinegar, sugar, and salt and bring to a boil over medium-high heat. Cook, stirring, until the sugar has dissolved, then pour the mixture over the scallions. Let the scallions cool in the liquid.

When ready to serve, heat a large cast-iron skillet over high heat and, working in batches, cook the pork, turning the pieces often as they brown, until cooked through and tender, 12 to 15 minutes. Transfer the pork to a cutting board and roughly chop. Once you have cooked all of the pork, scrape the chopped pieces back into the skillet and let soak in its cooking juices. Meanwhile, remove the scallions from the pickling liquid and thinly slice them. Serve the pork while still warm with tortillas, pickled scallions, and toasted sesame seeds.

Hija de Sánchez

COPENHAGEN, DENMARK

No offense to Copenhagen—seriously, we love Copenhagen—but the Mexican food in the Danish capital is in such a state that if Taco Bell ever makes it there, it'd probably get a Michelin star. Well, not if Rosio Sánchez has anything to say about it. The former pastry chef at Noma, René Redzepi's rundown cat cafe, she struck out on her own with the taqueria Hija de Sánchez, where she channels her perfectionist impulses into the pretense-free food she ate as a kid in Chicago.

In Copenhagen, this is a feat at least as hard as Redzepi's making dinner with local spruce shoots and lichen. Tomatillos are too expensive to import. Her customers, although admirably enthusiastic, sometimes refer to tortillas as pancakes. She makes her own, including the masa, because that's her style but also because you can't buy freshly made masa and tortillas on the corner like you can in Little Village, the neighborhood where she grew up. Her tacos are simple but hard-won, from classics like carnitas, tongue, and chicken in mole to departures that taste like classics, like fried tiny Fjord shrimp or crispy fish skin. When she makes gooseberry salsa, it's not for novelty's sake, but because salsa made from tart fruit is awesome.

Tacos already make for such fine drinking food that Sánchez didn't need to switch up her flow when cooking for her mezcal-soaked friends. She did, however, teach us a trick for making a good thing even better: Before piling on slices of pork al pastor (you know, the chile-marinated pork with pineapple that is often cooked, gyro-like, on a vertical spit), she fuses tortillas with cheese by adding them dairy side down directly on a hot griddle. That's the "dirty" part. And if that's dirty, we don't want to be clean.

PASTOR PASTE

2 dried guajillo chiles, stemmed

1 dried ancho chile, stemmed

½ dried chipotle morita chile, stemmed

½ cup freshly squeezed lime juice

¼ cup plus 2 tablespoons achiote paste

¼ cup plus 2 tablespoons water

3 tablespoons packed dark brown sugar

2½ tablespoons fine sea salt

2½ tablespoons freshly ground black pepper

1 tablespoon plus 2 teaspoons apple cider vinegar

1 tablespoon dried oregano

¼ teaspoon ground cloves

7 bay leaves

3 garlic cloves, peeled

PORK AND PINEAPPLE

4½ pounds pork belly, skin removed, cut into ¼-inch- thick slices

1 small pineapple, peeled, cored, and cut into ¼-inch- thick slices

¼ cup olive oil

GUACACHILE

½ heaping packed cup roughly chopped fresh cilantro (stems and leaves), plus more for serving

⅓ cup freshly squeezed lime juice

1 tablespoon grapeseed oil

1 teaspoon fine sea salt

2 jalapeños, stemmed, seeded, and roughly chopped

½ ripe avocado, pitted and peeled

½ garlic clove, peeled

¼ medium white onion, roughly chopped

FOR SERVING

1¼ pounds queso fresco, finely crumbled

3 dozen 6-inch corn or flour tortillas

1 white onion, finely chopped

½ bunch fresh cilantro, roughly chopped

Dirty Al Pastor Tacos with Guacachile   SERVES 8 TO 10

To make the pastor paste, combine the guajillo, ancho, and chipotle chiles in a small bowl and pour in boiling water to cover. Let soak for 20 minutes. Drain and discard the water, then transfer the chiles to a blender along with the remaining marinade ingredients. Blend until smooth, then scrape into a very large bowl. Add the pork belly and toss to coat the pork evenly, then cover the bowl with plastic wrap and refrigerate for at least 24 hours or up to 3 days.

Prepare a grill for direct, high-heat grilling, or heat a grill pan over high. Remove the pork belly slices from the marinade and wipe off as much of the marinade as you can with your hands. Grill the meat in batches if necessary, until caramelized and tender, about 8 minutes, flipping the slices once halfway through. Transfer to a platter and tent with foil to keep warm.

After the pork has been grilled, in a large bowl, toss the pineapple with the olive oil. Add the pineapple slices to the grill and cook, flipping once, until lightly charred on both sides, about 4 minutes. Transfer the pineapple to a cutting board and roughly chop, then scatter the pineapple over the pork.

To make the guacachile, combine all of the ingredients along with 2 tablespoons water in a blender or food processor and puree until silky smooth.

Heat a nonstick skillet or griddle over medium. To make each taco, add 1 tablespoon of the cheese directly to the skillet, cover with a tortilla, and cook until the cheese is golden brown, 1 to 2 minutes. Using a flat spatula, scrape off the cheese together with the tortilla and flip the tortilla with cheese onto a plate. Top with grilled pork belly and pineapple. Spoon on some guacachile and sprinkle with chopped onion and cilantro.

Momofuku Milk Bar

NEW YORK, NEW YORK

Christina Tosi's greatest strength is her palate. And what's propelled the visionary behind Milk Bar, the Momofuku sweets spinoff, to the top of the sugar heap (and a gig as a *Master Chef* judge) is that this palate isn't sensitive to the nuances in various chocolate varietals; rather, it's attuned to the pure nostalgic joy of French fries dunked in a milkshake. Whether you realized it or not, that salty-sweet, hot-cold delight was probably your first experience with culinary sophistication.

Her best desserts are moderately deranged riffs on iconic, glorious junk: like insanely delicious crack pie (think pecan pie without the pecans) and compost cookies (which contain chocolate and butterscotch, pretzels and potato chips). She cooks like a twelve-year-old who has spent too much time at Dairy Queen—but in the best way possible.

So when she undertook a day-drinking adventure, her crew of Wonderwomen headed out in a van stocked with kimchi Bloody Marys directly through the Holland Tunnel to the closest DQ. After a breakfast of Blizzard, fries, and chicken strips, her nostalgia tour continued at Brooklyn's Rockaway Beach, where kites were flown, cutthroat sandcastle-building competitions were had, and kimchi micheladas were downed, and then putt-putt golf on Randall's Island. Tosi is just as sweet as her signature cereal milk, but she takes her fun very seriously. And so do her friends: midway through a game, Mission Chinese Food chef Danny Bowien delivered several dozen Taco Bell Doritos Locos Tacos. Putt-putt gave way to a fever dream of tailgating fare, like kimchi quesadillas, seven-layer dip, and grilled ham and cheese sandwiches with sweet corn cookies standing in for bread. The cheese was American, of course, and one of her friends carried around the yellow block like it was Simba on Pride Rock. It was all fun and games until someone called the cops.

When Christina Tosi isn't in sweets mode, making birthday-cake shakes and cornflake-and-marshmallow cookies, she cooks glories like this seven-layer dip. Don't let the simplicity of this recipe fool you—the details are important. You must, for instance, use iceberg lettuce. You really should buy canned refried beans instead of attempting to make your own. (Because it's seven-layer dip.) And you should eat it nice and cold, as if you've pulled it straight from the fridge during a bout of desperate hunger, which you probably have. The only part that requires cooking is when you whip up classic "taco beef," cooking the meat with some spices, though we doubt Tosi would mind if you used a seasoning packet. She might even give you a high five.

Seven-Layer Dip   SERVES 20

TACO BEEF

3 tablespoons vegetable oil

2 pounds ground beef

2 tablespoons chili powder

1½ tablespoons ground cumin

1½ teaspoons paprika

1½ teaspoons crushed red pepper flakes

1½ teaspoons kosher salt

¾ teaspoon garlic powder

¾ teaspoon onion powder

¾ teaspoon dried oregano, preferably Mexican

DIP

1 tablespoon vegetable oil

2 (15-ounce) cans refried pinto beans

Kosher salt and freshly ground black pepper

2 (16-ounce) containers sour cream

4 ripe avocados, halved, pitted, and peeled

Freshly squeezed juice of 2 limes

8 vine-ripe tomatoes, cored and diced

½ head iceberg lettuce, cored and shredded (about 4 cups)

1½ cups shredded Mexican cheese blend (or equal parts cheddar and Monterey Jack cheese)

Tortilla chips, for serving

To make the taco beef, heat the oil in a large saucepan or skillet over medium-high, then add the beef and cook, stirring to break it up, until it is no longer pink, about 10 minutes. Add all the remaining ingredients and keep cooking, stirring, until all the liquid evaporates and the beef is lightly browned, about 5 minutes more. Take the pan off the heat and let the beef cool completely.

To make the dip, heat the oil in a large skillet over medium-high heat until it shimmers. Add the beans and cook, stirring, until smooth and spreadable, about 3 minutes. Season with salt and pepper, remove from the heat, and let cool completely.

Add the beans to a 9 by 13-inch baking dish and spread to form an even layer. Top with the sour cream in an even layer, then the beef in an even layer. Mash the avocados and lime juice together in a bowl, season with salt and pepper, then spread this evenly over the beef. Top with the tomatoes in an even layer, then the lettuce and the cheese. Cover with plastic wrap and refrigerate until the dip is thoroughly chilled, at least 2 hours or up to 24 hours. Serve with tortilla chips.

CHAPTER 4

Hardcore

ANDREW MCCONNELL

Chef's Night Out usually has a star, and it's not always the chef. So even though Andrew McConnell is a big reason we dig dining in Melbourne, one of his friends totally stole the show. It makes sense, since McConnell is that rare bird who runs multiple, influential restaurants (Cumulus Inc. and Supernormal, to name two) and puts out a cookbook but prefers to dodge the spotlight. We were lucky he agreed to let us tag along in the first place.

Perhaps acknowledging his own penchant for chilling in the cut, McConnell brought Frank Valvo, who has the opposite preference. He's the creator of where-all-the-artists-go salon Fur Hairdressing, dead ringer for Mike from *Twin Peaks* (except for the missing arm), and the man who decided that a group of chefs, McConnell included, strolling down the street in a pack should go by the title "One Erection: The Oldest Boy Band in Town." When they made it back to Cumulus's wine bar, Frank finally got to make the dish he'd been talking about for an entire year. While McConnell whipped up mushrooms on toast—with porcinis as big as your head—and waffles with caviar (or more appropriately, caviar with waffles), Frank lived his dream, breading and deep-frying Camembert cheese, then drizzling it with maple syrup. Under the watchful eye of McConnell, a killer collabo was born—the slightly stinky, oozy cheese made even oozier, encased in a crunchy shell. If McConnell is Harry Styles, Frank is so Zayn.

Deep-Fried Camembert   SERVES 2 TO 4

⅓ cup heavy cream

1 large egg

3 tablespoons all-purpose flour

1¼ cup panko breadcrumbs

1 (9-ounce) wheel camembert, cut into 6 equal wedges

Canola oil, for deep frying

Kosher salt

Maple syrup, for serving

In a medium bowl, whisk together the cream and the egg. Put the flour and breadcrumbs in 2 separate bowls. Working with 1 wedge at a time, add the camembert to the flour and toss to coat lightly, dunk it in the egg mixture, and add to the breadcrumbs and toss to coat well. Set the wedges on a plate as they're breaded.

Heat 2 inches of oil in a large saucepan to 400°F. Line a plate with paper towels. Working in batches to avoid crowding the oil, fry the wedges until golden, about 1 minute. Using a slotted spoon, transfer them to the paper towels and season with salt. Serve immediately with maple syrup.

Kadeau

BORNHOLM, DENMARK

Kadeau is *that* place. To get there, you have to make your way to the Danish island of Bornholm, in the middle of the Baltic Sea, a three-hour ferry ride from Copenhagen. The place is so goddamn picture perfect, a small cottage made almost entirely of windows a short walk on soft sand from the beach. It's the kind of place you want so badly to make fun of—where you'll occasionally get a plate filled mostly with inedible tree branches or stones—but where full-on flavor makes up for the pageantry. No wonder Kadeau inspires whispers among the food illuminati that it's even better than you-know-where.

The Dane behind the stove, Nicolai Nørregaard, and his buddies Rasmus Kofoed and Magnus Høeg Kofoed (not related) are all native Bornholmers, so their adventure began on the island. They visited a friend's restaurant to sip spruce-flavored aquavit and spirits made from wild apples in the middle of the goddamn forest. They rolled by a seaside smokehouse to grab herring and beers for the ferry ride to Copenhagen, because that's how they roll. They walked the streets, wine bottle in hand, until they found Distortion, the city's annual EDM party, where they channeled their inner Eurotrash with Jäger shots.

Don't be fooled: they might spend their days foraging for wild leaves, setting hay on fire, and tweezering wood ants (caught by one of their dads) onto half moons of celeriac, but drunk cravings are universal. Proof: the tray of twice-baked potatoes they hauled from the oven late night, crisp skinned and filled with a combo of bacon, cheddar, and broccoli.

NICOLAI NØRREGAARD

6 large russet potatoes

1 pound bacon, cut into ½-inch pieces

Kosher salt and freshly ground black pepper

1 (5-ounce) head broccoli, florets cut into small pieces, stalk peeled and cut into ½-inch dice

1 cup crème fraîche

4 tablespoons unsalted butter, at room temperature

8 ounces extra-sharp cheddar cheese, cut into ½-inch cubes, at room temperature

½ cup thinly sliced chives

Stuffed Jacket Potatoes MAKES 12

Heat the oven to 450°F. Using a fork, poke holes all over the potatoes. Put the potatoes on a rimmed baking sheet and bake until tender when pierced in the center with a fork, about 1 hour.

While the potatoes bake, scatter the bacon in a large skillet, set it over medium-high heat, and cook, stirring occasionally, until the fat renders and the bacon is crisp, 8 to 10 minutes. Using a slotted spoon, transfer the bacon to paper towels to drain, reserving the fat for another use.

Bring a medium saucepan of salted water to a boil, add the broccoli, and cook until just crisp-tender, 30 to 60 seconds. Drain the broccoli in a colander and let cool.

Remove the potatoes from the oven and decrease the oven temperature to 375°F. Let the potatoes sit until cool enough to handle, then halve each potato lengthwise. Using a spoon, carefully scoop out the flesh, leaving a ¼-inch-thick layer inside the skin, and transfer it to a large bowl. Add the crème fraîche and butter and mash until smooth. Add the bacon, broccoli, cheese, and chives and stir well. Season to taste with salt and pepper. Put the potato-skin shells back on the baking sheet, skin-side down, and divide the potato mixture among them, mounding it up.

Using the tines of a fork, rough up the top of each potato to form nooks and crannies, which will get crispy in the oven. Bake the stuffed potatoes until the tops are golden brown and the cheese is melted, 15 to 20 minutes. Serve while hot.

Poutine Your Way

NEW YORK, NEW YORK; AUSTIN, TEXAS;
AND LOS ANGELES, CALIFORNIA

There's a certain inevitability to poutine, Canada's national dish and now beloved far and wide. Its birth—in the late 1950s or early '60s, according to whose creation story you trust—came when some sage soul eating French fries had access to both brown gravy and cheese curds, and thought, *Hey, these would all be better together*. All these years later, poutine has officially gone through all three phases of culinary lionization. First there is boutique-ification (for example, the many *poutineries* that gussy up the classic formula), then McDonald's-ification (fast-food chains across Canada offer industrial facsimiles), then lip balm (so went bacon; so goes poutine).

It's certainly not the only way cooks around the world dress up the noble French fry. (See Peruvian *lomo saltado*, where beef stir-fry takes the place of cheese and gravy, and disco fries, the Northern New Jersey diner specialty that's like an even-less-classy poutine). But it is quintessential drinking food—gluttonous, crispy-soggy-salty, booze-absorbing master-piece, the most delicious thing to come out of Canada since Ryan Gosling (meow!).

And like Ryan, poutine has range. So we invited three of the chefs who wisely chose *poutine* to conclude their debauched nights to share recipes for poutine done their way.

Noah Bernamoff, whose Mile End Deli brought Montreal-style bagels and smoked meat sandwiches to New York, sticks to the classic: crunchy fries and squeaky curds doused with roux-thickened chicken gravy.

Arjun and Nakul Mahendro, the Toronto-born brothers behind the L.A. gastropub Badmaash (it means "bad-ass" in Hindi), go Canada on the bottom and Punjabi (chicken tikka masala!) on top. If you want to add paneer, you should—it's basically the Indian version of cheese curds.

Callie Speer, who was born and raised in Austin and nowadays runs the diner of our dreams called Bombshell, got really weird, and we loved it. She made a poutine buffet, setting out, among other things, this incredible stewed goat shoulder, whipping up coffee-spiked red-eye gravy (Texas, what what!), and serving an array of cheeses—Cotija, blue cheese, and, um, orange cheese.

GRAVY

4 tablespoons unsalted butter

¼ cup finely chopped shallots (about 2 small shallots)

Kosher salt

2 tablespoons all-purpose flour

2 cups low-sodium chicken broth

Freshly ground black pepper

FRIES

Vegetable oil, for deep frying

2 pounds large russet potatoes, scrubbed clean and cut into ½-inch sticks, then soaked in cold water until ready to fry

Kosher salt

2 cups (10 ounces) cheese curds, at room temperature

Classic Poutine   SERVES 6

To make the gravy, melt the butter in a medium saucepan over medium heat. Add the shallots, season with a pinch of salt, and cook, stirring occasionally, until softened, about 5 minutes. Sprinkle the flour over the shallots and whisk until the flour has a toasty aroma and turns light brown, about 2 minutes. Slowly pour in the chicken broth while whisking constantly, then continue to whisk until smooth. Simmer until the gravy thickens and the flavors meld, about 20 minutes. Taste and season with additional salt and pepper.

To make the fries, heat 4 inches of oil in a large saucepan until a deep-fry thermometer reaches 275°F to 300°F. Line a baking sheet with paper towels. Drain the potatoes and pat them dry. Working in batches to avoid crowding the oil, fry the potatoes until they go from shiny to matte, 3 to 5 minutes. This is just the first frying; don't worry! Use a strainer to transfer them to the prepared baking sheet.

When you've fried all the potatoes, fry them again: Heat the oil to 350°F and line a second baking sheet with paper towels. Fry the potatoes in batches until they're golden brown and crispy on the outside but soft and chewy on the inside, 4 to 5 minutes. Transfer them to the prepared baking sheet to drain and immediately toss with plenty of salt.

To assemble the poutine, sprinkle about a quarter of the cheese curds in the bottom of a serving dish and top with the hot fries. Evenly spread the remaining cheese curds over them and pour the gravy generously over the fries. Eat right away.

CALLIE SPEER

SLOW-COOKED GOAT

1 tablespoon vegetable oil

2½ pounds boneless
goat shoulder

Kosher salt and freshly
ground black pepper

1 pound Roma tomatoes,
cored and chopped

½ cup pitted Castelvetrano
olives, chopped

4 carrots, quartered

1 leek, sliced into 3-inch
segments and well-cleaned

1½ cups dry red wine

6 cups low-sodium chicken
broth or vegetable, plus
more if needed

½ bunch fresh thyme

½ bunch fresh rosemary

REDEYE GRAVY

¼ cup rendered bacon fat
or lard

½ cup all-purpose flour

¾ teaspoon Tabasco sauce

½ lemon

1 tablespoon instant coffee
powder

1 (2-pound) bag frozen
French fries or tater tots

1 cup shredded Monterey
Jack cheese

4 to 6 poached eggs
(optional)

Goat Poutine with Redeye Gravy   SERVES 4 TO 6

To cook the goat, heat the oven to 300°F. Heat the oil in a Dutch oven or a similar oven-safe pot over high until it begins to smoke. Season the goat liberally with salt and pepper and sear until evenly browned all over, 8 to 10 minutes. Transfer to a plate and set aside.

Add the tomatoes, olives, carrots, and leek to the oil and cook, stirring frequently, until soft, 5 to 7 minutes. Pour in the wine and let it come to a simmer, scraping the pot to loosen anything stuck to the bottom. Simmer until the liquid reduces slightly, 2 to 3 minutes. Add the stock, let it boil, then add the goat and let the liquid boil again.

Cover tightly and cook in the oven until the goat pulls apart easily, 3 to 4 hours. Add the thyme and rosemary, re-cover, and continue cooking in the oven for another 20 minutes. Uncover and let cool to room temperature.

Remove the goat from pot, reserving the liquid, and shred, à la pulled pork. Transfer the meat to a saucepan to keep warm. Strain the liquid and transfer it to a medium pot. Boil it over high heat until it's reduced to about 3 cups. (If you don't have enough braising liquid, use chicken broth to get to 3 cups.)

Meanwhile, bake the French fries or tots according to package directions.

To make the gravy, heat the bacon fat in a medium saucepan over medium-high heat until it shimmers. Add the flour and cook, stirring constantly, until the flour taste and texture are gone, about 2 minutes. Add the reduced braising liquid, the Tabasco, and a good squeeze of lemon juice and cook, whisking, until thick. If you want, add a little more lemon juice to taste. Strain through a fine-mesh strainer into a bowl and whisk in the instant coffee until it dissolves.

To assemble, top the warm fries or tots with the goat meat, gravy, cheese, and eggs. Eat right away.

CHICKEN TIKKA

1 cup plain yogurt

1 tablespoon minced garlic

1 tablespoon paprika

1 teaspoon minced ginger

Kosher salt and freshly ground black pepper

Cayenne pepper (optional)

4 or 5 medium boneless, skinless chicken thighs, trimmed of excess fat

FRIES

Vegetable oil, for deep frying

5 medium russet potatoes, scrubbed clean and cut into ½-inch sticks, then soaked in cold water until ready to fry

Paprika, for seasoning

Salt

2 cups (10 ounces) cheese curds

1½ cups canned poutine gravy (preferably St. Hubert brand), or see the gravy recipe for Classic Poutine, page 101

Handful roughly chopped fresh cilantro

Chicken Tikka Poutine

SERVES 6

To prepare the chicken tikka, in a large bowl, stir together the yogurt, garlic, paprika, and ginger and season with salt and pepper. Add cayenne to taste if you want some spiciness. Add the chicken and toss to coat. Cover and refrigerate at least 4 hours and up to overnight.

To make the fries, heat 4 inches of oil in a large saucepan until a deep-fry thermometer reaches 325°F. Line a baking sheet with paper towels. Drain the potatoes and pat them dry. Once the oil is hot, cook the fries in batches to avoid crowding the oil until they're pale yellow, about 3 minutes. This is just the first frying; don't worry! Use a strainer to transfer them to the prepared baking sheet.

When you're ready to finish the poutine, prepare a grill or grill pan for cooking with medium-high heat and rub the grates with a little oil so nothing sticks. Grill the chicken until charred and tender, 8 to 10 minutes, flipping halfway through. Let the chicken rest on a cutting board while you fry those fries for a second time.

Heat the oil to 375°F. While the oil is heating, heat your gravy in a small saucepan over medium heat.

Line a baking sheet with paper towels. Cook the fries in batches again until golden brown and crisp on the outside and soft on the inside, 4 to 5 minutes. Drain on the prepared baking sheet and immediately season with a little paprika and salt.

To assemble the poutine, mound the fries on a serving platter and sprinkle the cheese curds over them. Ladle on the hot gravy, making sure to cover every curd like a good poutine-ist.

Cut the chicken into cubes and sprinkle it and the cilantro onto the poutine. Eat immediately.

The Black Hoof

TORONTO, CANADA

Jen Agg is a boss. She runs a constellation of culinary greatness in Canada, including a Haitian-influenced spot in Montreal she launched with her artist husband and musical total-nobodies Win Butler and Régine Chassagne. (Psst: they're in Arcade Fire.) The oldest and brightest of these stars being the Black Hoof, where Torontonians go for their fix of bone marrow, horse tartare, and pig's ear slaw, plus incredibly fun, creative plates that—also incredibly—were turned out until recently on the kind of shitty electric stovetop you had in your first apartment. But she's a figurative boss, too—the kind of person elderly guys might call a real pistol. (You might consider reading her memoir, *I Hear She's a Real Bitch*.)

We had a grand time touring Toronto with the restaurant matriarch, scarfing tacos, downing hipster cocktails, and sipping sinuously smooth twenty-year-old Pappy Van Winkle. ("It's like a gentle, velvet strangulation," Agg said, clutching her throat). And we were thrilled that it concluded with nachos, or as Agg called it, "whitey Mexican food." Her recipe is, appropriately

for nachos, free of dogma and full of humility. You can use Vidalia onions "or whatever." You might do like she does and use green bell peppers ("I can't emphasize enough how unfancy these are"). You can hate on her addition of shredded lettuce ("I don't care; I love lettuce on nachos"). Our favorite part about this messy, shovel-into-your-mouth dish is her nose-to-tail tweak. It's also our only source of disagreement. Describing the chili that makes her nachos extra good as "like regular chili, but with tongue," she understates her own genius. Fatty, inexpensive tongue makes for a particularly rich, beefy result—though, sure, ground beef works just fine. We don't want to end up on her bad side, so while she says "I don't think anyone is going to make tongue chili ever," we say: prove her wrong.

TONGUE CHILI

2 tablespoons vegetable oil

2 pounds ground beef tongue (ask your butcher to do this for you) or ground beef or veal

2 tablespoons chili powder

2 teaspoons dried oregano

2 teaspoons ground cumin

1 tablespoon all-purpose flour

1½ cups beef stock

Kosher salt and freshly ground black pepper

NACHOS

1 (12-ounce) bag tortilla chips

1 lime

Kosher salt

1 (15-ounce) container pico de gallo, drained thoroughly

1 teaspoon agave syrup

2 cups shredded cheddar cheese

1 cup shredded Monterey Jack cheese

⅓ cup diced yellow onion

⅓ cup diced green bell peppers

3 cups shredded iceberg lettuce

1 cup sour cream

Tongue Chili Nachos   SERVES 12

To make the tongue chili, heat the oil in a large saucepan over medium-high until it shimmers. Add the tongue and cook, stirring, until golden brown, about 8 minutes. Add the chili powder, oregano, and cumin, and cook, stirring, until fragrant, about 1 minute. Add the flour and cook for 1 minute, then stir in the stock, scraping the bottom to release any stuck-on bits. Once the stock comes to a boil, reduce the heat to maintain a simmer, and cook, stirring occasionally, until thickened, about 6 minutes. Remove the chili from the heat and season with salt and pepper.

To make the nachos, heat the oven to 425°F. Spread the chips out in more or less one layer on a rimmed baking sheet. Finely grate the zest of half of the lime over the chips and sprinkle them with salt. Top evenly with the chili. Stir the pico de gallo and agave syrup together in a small bowl, then dollop over the chips. Evenly sprinkle on both cheeses, then the onion and peppers. Bake until the cheese is melted and the chips are lightly toasted at the edges, about 10 minutes.

Remove the nachos from the oven, then sprinkle with the lettuce. Zest the rest of the lime into a bowl, squeeze in its juice, add the sour cream, and stir to combine. Dollop the lime sour cream over the nachos and serve while hot.

Best Pizza

BROOKLYN, NEW YORK

On the very first episode of *Chef's Night Out*, David Chang said it best: When we're good and drunk, few of us crave oxtail or bone marrow. We want a crappy slice of pizza that we won't even remember eating. Judging from the many pies with which chefs capped their nights out, Chang was right—except perhaps for the "crappy" part.

To celebrate the joys of post-midnight pizza consumption, we enlisted the help of Frank Pinello, the host of *The Pizza Show* on MUNCHIES and the pizzaiolo behind Best Pizza, an unremarkable storefront on Havemeyer in Brooklyn that makes the platonic ideal of the pinnacle of pizza achievement—the New York slice. Pinello does things the old way. That's why his slices are everything. With a baby face and thick Bensonhurst accent, he's just a kid from deep Brooklyn who charmingly mangles words like "ricotta" (say it with him: "ri-GAWT") and lavishes only top-shelf ingredients on the unassuming pies that emerge from his wood-fired oven in four minutes flat. His is one of the pizzerias still fighting the good fight, that risk charging a little more rather than skimping on the good stuff.

Since you may not have a century-old wood oven (You don't? Slacker), Pinello shares his method for producing his finest pizza at home—crunchy, airy crust topped with barebones, perfect tomato sauce, and baked with a judicious sprinkling of fresh mozzarella.

All you need is a cheap pizza peel (come on, it's like $10), a heavy pizza stone (a splurge at about $40, but the only way to produce pizza worth eating at home), and the willingness to get your hands dirty. Of course, he's a practical man, so he's also totally down with buying dough at your favorite corner pizza place.

As Pinello would tell you, baking is a science, cooking is an art, and pizza falls somewhere in the middle. Once you've completed the relatively fastidious dough-making process, it's time to have fun, using that dough as a canvas for cravings. Get creative. Get nasty. But keep in mind some basic principles. If we can channel Pinello for a moment, toppings are awesome, but don't overload the pie—a little goes a long way. And as you top the pie, put lighter ingredients near the center of the pie and heavier stuff around the outside, because when the crust puffs up in the oven, it'll push everything toward the middle.

For home pizza-making purposes, we recommend using Pinello's dough and tomato sauce as a jumping-off point. Then do your thing, or do one of the things on page 115.

DOUGH

1½ cups warm water
(110 to 115°F)

1 teaspoon active dry yeast

1½ tablespoons olive oil,
plus more for the bowl

1½ teaspoons kosher salt

3 cups all-purpose flour,
plus more, if needed

SAUCE

1 (28-ounce) can whole
peeled tomatoes

1 tablespoon kosher salt

Pizza

MAKES DOUGH FOR 4 ROUND 10-INCH PIZZAS OR 2 GRANDMA-STYLE PIZZAS AND 3½ CUPS SAUCE

To make the dough, if kneading by hand, combine the water, yeast, olive oil, and salt in a medium bowl. If using a stand mixer, combine these ingredients in the stand-mixer bowl. Whisk to dissolve the yeast and salt, then let the yeast foam for 5 minutes.

Oil the inside of a large bowl. Add the flour to the yeast mixture and knead the dough with your hands or, if using a stand mixer, with the dough hook attachment until the dough is smooth and just slightly tack, but not sticky, at least 5 minutes. If the dough feels sticky, gradually knead in up to ½ cup more flour until it doesn't.

Put the dough in the oiled bowl, cover with plastic wrap, and put in a warm place to proof until doubled in size, about 1 hour. After proofing, divide the dough into 4 equal-sized balls if you're making 10-inch round pies or 2 equal-size balls if you're making grandma-style pies (see page 112). Transfer the balls to a baking sheet. Cover with plastic wrap and proof in a warm place for an additional hour, or until the balls double in size.

To freeze unused dough, place the balls on a plate, cover with plastic wrap, and place in the freezer until frozen through. Remove and transfer each ball to a separate plastic bag. Replace in the freezer and store for up to 3 months. The night before you want to make pizza, transfer the desire dough to the refrigerator to defrost. When completely defrosted, remove dough from the plastic bag, place on a baking sheet, and cover with plastic wrap. Leave in a warm places to proof for an additional hour, or until doubled in size.

To make the sauce, using a food mill, food processor, or your hands, crush the tomatoes until you have a slightly chunky puree. Stir in the salt. That's it! Store in an airtight container in the fridge for up to 5 days, or in the freezer for up to 3 months.

How to Make Pizza

10-INCH ROUND PIES, PIZZA STONE METHOD:
Put a pizza stone on the top rack of the oven
and preheat the broiler. Heat the stone for
at least 30 minutes. Working with one ball
of dough at a time and on a lightly floured
surface, use your fingertips or a rolling pin
to press the dough ball into a 10-inch circle,
about 1/8-inch thick. Top with your favorite
toppings. Carefully transfer the pizza to a
lightly floured pizza peel and slide it onto
the pizza stone in the oven. Bake until the
crust is golden and the cheese is bubbling,
about 10 minutes.

10-INCH ROUND PIES, CAST-IRON SKILLET METHOD:
Heat the oven to 500°F. Place a 12-inch cast-
iron skillet in the oven to warm for at least
15 minutes. Working with one ball of dough
at a time and on a lightly floured surface, use
your fingertips or a rolling pin to press the
dough ball into a 10-inch circle, about 1/8-inch
thick. Remove the cast-iron skillet from the
oven and carefully transfer the dough to it,
using your fingertips to spread the dough out
to the sides of the pan. Top with your favorite
toppings. Carefully transfer the skillet to the
oven and bake until the crust is golden and
the sauce is bubbling, about 10 minutes.

GRANDMA-STYLE PIES: To make a grandma-
style (aka rectangular) pizza, heat the oven
to 450°F with the racks positioned in the
top and bottom thirds of the oven. Grease
two 13 by 18-inch baking sheets with olive
oil. Spread one ball of the pizza dough into
each baking sheet and, using your fingertips,
press it into an even layer to fill the pan. Top
with your favorite toppings. Bake the pizzas,
rotating the baking sheets after 12 minutes,
until the cheese and crust are golden and
crispy, 10 to 12 minutes more. Remove from
the oven, cool slightly, cut into slices, and eat
immediately.

Alon Shaya's Pizza Enzo

MAKES 2 (10-INCH) PIZZAS OR
1 GRANDMA-STYLE PIZZA

Before Israeli-born chef Alon Shaya sold New Orleans on hummus, he was tossing dough at Domenica on Baronne Street, where he topped a particularly fine pie with cheese (mozz and Parm) and tomatoes (cooked and fresh), then had the good sense drape the result with mortadella (aka Italian bologna). We don't think he'd mind that we went rogue, sending the pizza into the oven with the mortadella, so the meat curls and chars.

2 pizza dough balls for 10-inch pies or 1 pizza dough ball for a grandma-style pie, shaped (see page 111 for the dough recipe and page 112 for shaping instructions)

⅔ cup tomato sauce (page 111)

8 ounces fresh mozzarella, thinly sliced

4 ounces thinly sliced mortadella, quartered

8 cherry tomatoes, halved

4 tablespoons grated parmesan cheese

2 teaspoons crushed red pepper flakes

Fresh basil leaves, for garnish

For each 10-inch pie, spread ⅓ cup of sauce on the shaped dough, leaving a 1-inch border. Top with half of the mozzarella, half of the mortadella, and half of the tomatoes. Sprinkle with 2 tablespoons of the Parmesan and 1 teaspoon of the red pepper flakes. Bake according to the pizza stone or cast-iron skillet method on page 112. Garnish with basil before serving.

For a grandma-style pie, drizzle the tomato sauce on the shaped dough, taking care not to cover the entire surface. Top with the mozzarella, mortadella, and tomatoes. Sprinkle with the Parmesan and red pepper flakes. Bake according to the baking sheet method on page 112. Garnish with basil before serving.

Michael White's "Josh Ozersky" Pizza

MAKES 2 (10-INCH) PIZZAS OR
1 GRANDMA-STYLE PIZZA

Ozersky was a food writer, in the same way Picasso is a doodler and Thomas Keller is a cook. Meat was his muse, the subject of his gonzo prose and the focus of his annual festival of flesh, Meatopia, that drew the best chefs in the business. As he liked to crack: "I only eat things with parents." NYC pasta king Michael White knew him well before Ozersky passed away in 2015. Near the end of White's night out, he made his friend this meat lover's special.

1 tablepoon olive oil

8 ounces fennel sausage, casings removed

⅔ cup tomato sauce (page 111)

2 pizza dough balls for 10-inch pies or 1 pizza dough ball for a grandma-style pie, shaped (see page 111 for the dough recipe and page 112 for shaping instructions)

2 ounces thick-cut sliced pepperoni

½ cup shredded mozzarella

Heat the olive oil in a large skillet over medium-high. Add the sausage and cook, breaking it up into small pieces, until the sausage is browned, about 10 minutes.

For each 10-inch pie, spread ⅓ cup of the sauce on the shaped dough, leaving a 1-inch border. Top with half of the sausage and half of the pepperoni. Sprinkle with half of the mozzarella cheese and bake according to the pizza stone or cast-iron skillet method on page 112.

For a grandma-style pie, drizzle the tomato sauce on the shaped dough, taking care not to cover the entire surface. Top with the sausage and pepperoni. Sprinkle with the mozzarella and bake according to the baking sheet method on page 112.

Kavita Meelu's Margherita

MAKES 2 (10-INCH) PIZZAS OR
1 GRANDMA-STYLE PIZZA

If you thought curbside cuisine in Berlin was all about currywurst, you should meet Kavita Meelu. Soon after the British-born Indian moved to Germany's capital, she became a sort of awesome-food advocate, commemorating the city's underappreciated immigrant cooks. When she showed us her Berlin, it was full of papaya salad and hand-pulled noodles. Yet like so many who indulged our cameras, she couldn't resist the siren song of pizza—specifically this pie with the sneaky heat of Thai chiles lurking in the sauce. If you're down for some of that heat, add some minced then mashed fresh Thai chiles the tomato sauce on page 111. Or do like we do when we're lazy and just hit the slices with Tabasco.

⅔ cup tomato sauce (page 111)

2 pizza dough balls for 10-inch pies or 1 pizza dough ball for a grandma-style pie, shaped (see page 111 for the dough recipe and page 112 for shaping instructions)

1 cup shredded mozzarella

2 tablespoons olive oil

Fresh basil leaves, for garnish

Tabasco sauce, for drizzling

For each 12-inch pie, spread ⅓ cup of the sauce on the shaped dough, leaving a 1-inch border. Sprinkle with half of the mozzarella and drizzle with 1 tablespoon of the olive oil. Bake according to the pizza stone or cast-iron skillet method on page 112. Garnish with basil and shake on Tabasco sauce before serving.

For a grandma-style pie, drizzle the tomato sauce on the shaped dough, taking care not to cover the entire surface. Sprinkle with the mozzarella and drizzle with the olive oil. Bake according to the baking sheet method on page 112. Garnish with basil and shake on Tabasco sauce before serving.

Paulie Gee's Hellboy

MAKES 2 (10-INCH) PIZZAS OR
1 GRANDMA-STYLE PIZZA

The Hellboy is a collaboration between Paul Giannone, of the beloved pizzeria Paulie Gee's, in Greenpoint, Brooklyn, and music industry dropout turned honey slinger and pizza intern Mike Kurtz. The story goes that Kurtz fell for chile-infused honey while traveling in Brazil, started attempting to make the stuff at home, and obviously, drizzled his experiments on pizza. During his apprenticeship, Kurtz brought in bottle of his spicy honey for Giannone to try, and a salty-sweet pizza triumph was born. After people started requesting the honey to-go, Kurtz knew he was onto something and Mike's Hot Honey (mikeshothoney.com) was born.

⅔ cup tomato sauce (page 111)

2 pizza dough balls for 10-inch pies or 1 pizza dough ball for a grandma-style pie, shaped (see page 111 for the dough recipe and page 112 for shaping instructions)

8 ounces fresh mozzarella, thinly sliced

4 ounces thinly sliced hot soppressata

4 tablespoons grated Parmesan cheese

Hot honey, for drizzling

For each 10-inch pie, spread ⅓ cup of sauce on the shaped dough, leaving a 1-inch border. Top with half of the mozzarella and half of the soppressata, then sprinkle with 2 tablespoons of the Parmesan. Bake according to the pizza stone or cast-iron skillet method on page 112. Drizzle with hot honey before serving.

For a grandma-style pie, drizzle the tomato sauce on the shaped dough, taking care not to cover the entire surface. Top with the mozzarella and the soppressata, then sprinkle with the Parmesan. Bake according to the baking sheet method on page 112. Drizzle with hot honey before serving.

CHAPTER 5

Noodles, Rice, and Grains

LEAH COHEN

Pig and Khao

NEW YORK, NEW YORK

Like a Bengal tiger bathing by mangroves or a condor taking flight, a chef too drunk to cook is a rare and beautiful sight. She will ask for a large pot not by name but by drawing a large circle in the air to indicate its size. She may need to be propped up so that she can sing to the shrimp in the fry pan. Some chefs turn in meta-performances on their *Chef's Night Out*. They've seen the show and take particular care not to make fools of themselves. Others take getting wasted seriously—the Canadians, in general, and Leah Cohen in particular. Bravo!

The chef becomes too drunk to cook by immediately breaking her cardinal rule: no shots. "Let's take these shots, bitches!" she'll command, before asking what's in them. She will take her taquitos with shots of Tanduay (Filipino rum) and wash down her spaetzle with Austrian wine, and there will be more drinks after that, but she will not remember. The drunk chef will eventually dance her way back to her Lower East Side restaurant, Pig and Khao, the culmination of the Jewish-Filipino chef's journey from college flunk-out to culinary school grad to fancy-kitchen drone to *Top Chef* contestant. The menu is so her—cribbed from her travels in Southeast Asia, with porcine nods to her mother's heritage—pork belly adobo and sizzling pork head sisig. It all, incidentally, eats very well with booze. "White girl pad thai" will appear, and though she will not have personally cracked any of the eggs, she will have hugged everyone on her staff who did.

Pad thai falls into two general categories: There's the kind Americans eagerly gobble from takeout containers in rainbow curry slingers across this great country, where the dish is so omnipresent you'd think it was the king of all Thai noodle dishes. And there's the rather spare rendition you find at specialized outfits in Thailand, where it's just one fine noodle dish among many. Leah Cohen's pad thai is a sort of midpoint between the two—with the comfortingly familiar qualities of the Americanized version and the complex sweet-tart thrill (from tamarind and palm sugar) and textural contrasts (peanuts and bean sprouts, fatty egg and slick noodles) of the real thing.

Pad Thai   SERVES 4

SAUCE

1 cup finely chopped, packed palm sugar (4 disks)

⅔ cup fish sauce

½ cup tamarind paste

¼ cup packed light brown sugar

PAD THAI

¼ cup rendered pork fat or vegetable oil

8 large shrimp (10 ounces), peeled and deveined

1 large egg

1 medium shallot, thinly sliced

10 ounces dried pad thai noodles, soaked in boiling water to cover for 5 minutes, then drained

2 ounces smoked tofu or extra-firm tofu, cut into ½-inch cubes

½ cup thinly sliced Chinese chives or regular chives, plus more for serving

¼ cup roughly chopped roasted peanuts, plus more for serving

¼ cup mung bean sprouts, plus more for serving

1 heaping tablespoon finely chopped fresh cilantro

1 teaspoon Thai shrimp paste

Pinch of crushed red pepper flakes

½ lime, plus 4 wedges for serving

To make the sauce, combine the palm sugar, fish sauce, tamarind paste, and brown sugar in a small pot and bring to a boil. Turn the heat down to medium-low and let it simmer, stirring frequently, for 15 minutes, then remove from the heat and let cool. Reserve ½ cup of the sauce for the pad thai and refrigerate the rest in an airtight container for up to 2 weeks.

To make the pad thai, in a large cast-iron pan, heat the pork fat over high until it's almost smoking. Cook the shrimp, stirring occasionally, until lightly browned on both sides and just cooked through, about 3 minutes. Transfer to a bowl, leaving the fat behind. Add the egg on one side of the pan and the shallots on the other side. Once the white of the egg starts to set, scramble the egg and mix with the shallots. Add the reserved ½ cup pad thai sauce, the noodles, and the tofu, and cook for 1 minute. Stir in the chives, peanuts, sprouts, cilantro, shrimp paste, and red pepper flakes, and cook until the noodles are tender, about 1 minute more. Remove from the heat, add the cooked shrimp, squeeze the lime half over the noodles, and stir to combine. Sprinkle on more chives, peanuts, and sprouts and serve with lime wedges alongside.

JEREMIAH STONE AND FABIAN VON HAUSKE

Contra

NEW YORK, NEW YORK

To the list of things we're grateful for—good health, good friends, good wine—let us add that we're grateful Jeremiah Stone and Fabian von Hauske never opened that ice cream shop. After bonding in culinary school and putting in time at top spots abroad—Le Chateaubriand in Paris for Stone, Scandi-sensations Noma and Fäviken for von Hauske—the two reunited in New York to get into the scoop game. Fortunately for us all, they didn't, because now we have double trouble on the Lower East Side.

With Contra, they gave the city the best food deal since Gray's Papaya—ambitious, Instagram-bait food via an ever-shifting set menu. (Without the sticker shock, you don't resent your lack of choice.) They changed the game, then up and did it again just two doors down. With Wildair, they gave the city the kind of chill, oddball wine bar that used to exist only across the Atlantic—and through sheer force of natural wines, uni-topped potato pancakes, and smoked cheddar–dusted tartare, it became the place every chef wants to go to. It's American food, which just means "everything, just the way we feel like doing it."

All this killing it, as you might imagine, takes work. In fact, hanging with Stone after a night of service felt kind of like grabbing drinks with a new dad. Both he and von Hauske went hard—the final count was twenty-five dishes consumed, including enough flesh to send Stone into "meat shock"—but only one of them pronounced himself "on the edge of glory" when he was actually on the threshold of sleep.

Stone kept saying he didn't want to doze off, only to do so in the back of the van after snacks the Wildair's Brooklyn doppelgänger, Four Horsemen, and a cameo by LCD Soundsystem front man James Murphy, one of its owners. Poor Stone told us he was made an object of fun by friends who assumed he was wasted rather than overtired.

He pried his eyes open for the encore back at Wildair, where he threw together a dish he nicknamed Chinese Bolognese: noodles with ground pork, scallion, Chinese bacon, and fermented black beans. "It's somewhere between Panda Express and authentic Chinese food," he told us. That's about as American as you can get.

2 pounds ground fatty pork

1 cup fermented
black beans

1 teaspoon ground cumin

1 teaspoon freshly ground
white pepper

1 large yellow onion, diced

10 whole cloves

4 whole star anise

1 pound Biangbiang
noodles, or fresh flat
wheat noodles about
1½-inches wide

2 tablespoons vegetable oil

¼ cup minced ginger

5 garlic cloves, minced

2 bunches scallions,
thinly sliced

1 bunch fresh cilantro,
finely chopped

1 bunch fresh garlic
chives or regular chives,
finely chopped

Kosher salt

2 cups mung bean sprouts

½ cup dried chiles de árbol

Chinese Drunken Noodles SERVES 6

Combine the pork, black beans, cumin, white pepper, half of the onion, and 1 cup water in a medium heavy-bottomed pot. Wrap the cloves and star anise in cheesecloth, tie to make a little sack, and add the sack to the pot. Bring the water to a boil, then reduce the heat to low, cover with the lid, and simmer, stirring occasionally, until the pork is very tender and saucy, about 2½ hours. Remove from the heat and discard the spice sack.

Bring a large pot of lightly salted water to a boil. Add the noodles and cook, stirring, until tender, about 3 minutes. Drain the noodles and set aside.

Meanwhile, heat the oil in a large skillet over medium-high heat. Add the remaining onion along with the ginger and garlic, and cook, stirring, until the onion is slightly softened, about 3 minutes. Stir in the braised pork and cook, stirring, until warmed through, about 5 minutes. Stir in the noodles, tossing to coat with the porky sauce, then stir in the scallions, cilantro, and chives. Season with salt and transfer to a large platter. Scatter the bean sprouts and chiles over the noodles and serve immediately.

wd~50

NEW YORK, NEW YORK

When Wylie Dufresne opened his legendary restaurant wd~50 on the Lower East Side, the culinary wizard brought the kind of food to America that until then was being cooked only in the mountains of Spain and comic books about the future. He's the guy who figured out how to fry hollandaise sauce, turn shrimp into grits, and turn "everything" bagels into ice cream. His intrepid cooking made him such a chef's chef that when he closed the restaurant due to rent increases brought about in part by the value that same restaurant brought to local real estate values, literally ever chef you've ever heard of flew into New York to throw him a surprise goodbye party.

He's also a guy who likes what he likes, prevailing sentiment be damned. He prefers meat from boutique farms and adores Popeye's chicken. He was an early adopter of trans-glutaminase (aka "meat glue") and remains a steadfast fan of Land O'Lakes brand American cheese. So when he cooked for his pals after a solid evening of boozing—the hard-working chef was not impressed when our cameraman

passed out on the hood of a Chrysler minivan, which, for the record, barely even has a hood—his dish had the fridge-clearing feel of good, honest drunk food. There's leftover chicken for heft. There's shiitake mushrooms for umami. There's breadcrumbs for crunch. The only bit of high-techery comes from the bag of ice-cold peas, which are preserved in their frozen state by the molecular gastronomists at Birds Eye right after they're picked and are therefore frozen, Dufresne thinks, especially "pea-licious."

2½ cups frozen peas

Kosher salt and freshly
ground black pepper

5 tablespoons unsalted
butter

1 pound fresh shiitake
mushrooms, stemmed and
thinly sliced

1 tablespoon sherry vinegar

1 cup panko breadcrumbs

8 ounces dried gemelli
pasta

1½ cups roughly chopped
meat from a rotisserie
chicken

2 tablespoons extra-virgin
olive oil

Grated Parmesan cheese,
for serving

Torn mint leaves,
for serving

Gemelli Pasta with Peas, Chicken, and Mushrooms SERVES 4 TO 6

Combine 1½ cups of the peas and 1 cup water in a blender and blend until very smooth, adding more water if necessary to help blend. Season with salt and pepper.

Melt 3 tablespoons of the butter in a large skillet over medium-high heat. Add the mushrooms, 1 tablespoon water, and season with salt. Cook, stirring, until tender and slightly caramelized, about 10 minutes. Transfer the mushrooms to a bowl, season with the sherry vinegar and salt and set aside.

Wipe the pan clean and melt the remaining 2 tablespoons butter in the skillet over medium-high heat. Add the panko and cook, stirring, until a shade darker and crunchy, 3 to 4 minutes. Transfer to a separate bowl and set aside.

Bring a large pot of generously salted water to a boil. Add the pasta and cook until al dente, about 12 minutes. Drain, reserving 1 cup of the pasta water. Return the pasta to the pot along with the remaining 1 cup of peas, the chicken, the mushrooms, and 2 cups of the pea sauce. Add enough reserved pasta water to loosen the sauce, add the olive oil, and toss well to coat. Season with salt and pepper.

To serve, divide the pasta among bowls. Top with the breadcrumbs, Parmesan cheese, and mint leaves. Eat right away.

It's hard to believe, but Michael White barely eats pasta anymore. The once Falstaffian chef has dropped an entire adult human's worth of body-weight in the last five years, in part by cutting down to one bowl of the good stuff per week. We must've caught him on that happy day, because when we met up with him, he and his entourage—composed almost entirely of fat men named Josh (including the much-missed Ozersky, RIP)—piled into a Queens-bound SUV to eat at the legendary Thai restaurant Sripraphai. There, after analyzing the glaze on a pad thai and pronouncing it perfect, he proceeded to eat the place out of house and home (or at least out of deep-fried watercress salad). White and the Joshes did the kind of damage that you'd expect from men who regularly discuss strategies that allow eating significantly more than is probably advisable. Like the "air bath," where you step outside halfway through a meal to aid digestion, and the purely aspirational "neck transplant," which deals with the consequences.

Like the good Midwestern boy he is, White makes this monster carbonara with heavy cream, bacon, and a shitload of cheese (plus a handful of arugula, to ward off the scurvy). If you're Michael White, you can grab fresh tagliatelle from your restaurant kitchen on your way home; if you're not, he won't judge you for using dried. Either way, it's the kind of pasta you eat when no one's looking.

¾ cup heavy cream

4 large egg yolks

¼ cup olive oil

8 ounces bacon, cut into ½-inch pieces

4 garlic cloves, thinly sliced

1 pound fresh tagliatelle

A few handfuls of arugula

Freshly ground black pepper

½ cup grated Pecorino Romano or Parmesan cheese, plus more for serving

Late-Night Carbonara   SERVES 4

Bring a large pot of generously salted water to a boil. (It should be salty like the sea.)

Meanwhile, stir together the cream and egg yolks in a small bowl and set aside. Heat the olive oil in a large skillet over medium-high heat, add the bacon, and cook until lightly crisped, about 4 minutes. Add the garlic and cook until fragrant, about 2 minutes more. Remove the skillet from the heat.

When the water comes to a boil, cook the tagliatelle, stirring, until al dente, about 3 minutes. Drain the pasta, reserving about 1 cup of the pasta water. Return the skillet with the bacon and garlic to medium heat and add the pasta, enough reserved water to loosen the pasta, and the egg mixture, tossing to coat. Toss in the arugula, black pepper to taste, and the cheese. Serve immediately with more cheese and black pepper.

Brooklyn Star

BROOKLYN, NEW YORK

You might expect the chef who helped David Chang launch the Momofuku empire to be off running some minimalist restaurant, charging $150 for ramen-focused tasting menus or at least courting venture capital for a Korean burrito bowl startup. Not Quino Baca. "It was gonna be big; it was gonna be huge!" he said about Momofuku. "And I wanted to keep things small."

Instead of cashing in on a trend, he decided to do his own thing, opening an ode to Texas in Williamsburg, Brooklyn. The local beard patrol—and yes, that includes some of the worker bees milling around at MUNCHIES HQ—doesn't always register glimpses of the cheffy technique that elevates dishes like sweet tea-glazed chicken and country-fried steak from comfort food to really, really good comfort food. And we suspect that's just how Baca likes it.

Baca moved around as a kid—his dad was in the foreign service—but he always had family in the Lone Star State. He went there often enough that it became the place that felt most like home. When he hit the town, he was drawn to spots that offered a similar sense of place. He ate Spam musubi—that's canned meat served in mutant sushi roll form—at Suzume, a joint a block away from Brooklyn Star that's run by former Noodle Bar alum Mikey Briones and inspired by his love of the mall food in his home state of Hawaii. At Peking Duck House, a beacon of Old New York that serves classic Chinatown fare with not a beard in sight, he had the crisp-skinned namesake. When he went in on shots and brews, he did so at Harefield Road, which is also within spitting distance of Brooklyn Star and in Brooklyn qualifies as a dive bar. Sufficiently loose, we headed back to the restaurant for sweet-spot fare: fried chicken, mac and cheese, biscuits, and collard greens. The kind of stuff we all crave at midnight. There was notably no kimchi in sight.

Baca's mac and cheese kills it. There's bacon. There's the hollow, spiral pasta called cavatappi (so much better than macaroni). There's Mornay sauce, better known as creamy cheese sauce—in this case spiked with both cheddar for deliciousness and processed stuff for superior melt factor. And there's the way the cast-iron skillet you cook it in creates those incredible crispy bits on the sides and bottom that'll cause fork fights at the table. Nothing else is necessary, but that's not to say we're hating on Baca's addition of peppery Texas-style cream gravy, which it turns out is just as good in this context as it is on country-fried steaks.

JOAQUIN BACA

GRAVY

1½ cups whole milk

1 bay leaf

1 sprig fresh thyme

2 tablespoons unsalted butter

¼ cup all-purpose flour

½ teaspoon kosher salt

½ teaspoon freshly ground black pepper

CHEESE SAUCE

½ cup (1 stick) unsalted butter

½ cup all-purpose flour

3 cups whole milk

1 cup heavy cream

2 tablespoons dry mustard powder

1 tablespoon mild hot sauce, such as Frank's Red Hot

1¼ pounds sharp white cheddar cheese, preferably Cabot, shredded

4 ounces processed cheese product, such as Velveeta, cubed

4 strips bacon

1 pound dried cavatappi or elbow macaroni

Kosher salt and freshly ground black pepper

Bacon-and-Gravy Mac and Cheese   SERVES 6 TO 8

To make the gravy, combine the milk, bay leaf, and thyme in a small saucepan and bring to a boil. Pour into a bowl and let steep for 30 minutes. Wipe the pan clean, add the butter, then return the pan to low heat. When the butter starts to foam, add the flour and cook, whisking constantly, until lightly toasted, about 10 minutes. Remove the herbs from the milk and discard them, then pour the milk into the saucepan, whisking constantly, bring to a simmer, and cook until smooth and thickened, about 5 minutes. Season with the salt and pepper, then remove from the heat and keep warm.

To make the cheese sauce, heat the butter in a large saucepan over low heat. When the butter starts to foam, add flour and cook, whisking constantly, until lightly toasted, about 10 minutes. Pour in the milk and cream, whisking constantly. Bring to a boil, then reduce the heat to maintain a steady simmer, and cook, stirring often, until thickened, about 10 minutes. Stir in the mustard powder and hot sauce, then add 1 pound of the cheddar and all of the cheese product and stir until melted and smooth. Remove the sauce from the heat and keep warm.

To make the mac and cheese, heat the oven to 400°F. Heat a 12-inch cast-iron skillet over medium heat, add the bacon strips, and cook, turning once, until they're crisp, about 10 minutes. Transfer the bacon to paper towels, reserving the bacon fat for another use (do not wipe out the skillet). Remove the skillet from the heat. Crumble the bacon into small pieces, then return them to the skillet. Bring a large pot of salted water to a boil, add the pasta, and cook until the pasta is tender but still crunchy, 5 to 6 minutes. Drain the pasta, then stir it into the cheese sauce. Season with salt and pepper.

Pour the macaroni and cheese over the bacon and smooth the top. Pour the gravy over the macaroni and cheese and spread it evenly over the top. Sprinkle on the remaining ¼ pound cheddar, then bake until bubbling and golden brown on top, about 35 minutes. Let cool for 10 minutes before serving.

Josh Kulp and Christine Cikowski's restaurant was born the day they hit on the shocking realization that if you make really good fried chicken and serve it with whipped butter seasoned with honey, people just might lose their minds over it. So they opened a place with the admirably direct title Honey Butter Fried Chicken, in Chicago's Avondale neighborhood. When they were making their MUNCHIES meal, they pulled out an old family meal favorite, merging two champions of the leftovers game—rice and fried chicken. The heat of a hot pan resurrects them both, while peanuts add crunch, pickled ramps add acid, and peas make the whole thing 100 percent healthy.

PICKLED RAMPS

1 pound ramps (or scallions), thoroughly cleaned, roots trimmed

½ cup white wine vinegar, rice vinegar, or a combination

⅓ cup water

1 tablespoon sugar

1 teaspoon kosher salt

1 teaspoon whole black peppercorns

1 teaspoon whole coriander seeds

1 teaspoon fennel seeds

FRIED RICE

1 large egg

Kosher salt

¼ cup peanut oil or other neutral oil

1 tablespoon soy sauce

1 tablespoon mirin

1 teaspoon minced ginger

1 teaspoon minced garlic

½ cup diced smoked country ham, preferably Benton's

¼ cup thinly sliced ramp greens or scallion greens

2 pieces leftover fried chicken, bones removed, diced

2 cups cooked basmati rice, chilled

½ cup fresh shelled peas (or defrosted frozen peas)

⅓ cup roasted salted peanuts, chopped

Fried Chicken Fried Rice SERVES 4

To make the pickled ramps, cut the green tops from the ramps, reserving them for the fried rice. Put the remaining parts (the white bulbs and pink stems) in a heatproof container with a lid or a large glass jar. Bring the rest of the ingredients to a boil in a small saucepan, then pour the hot liquid over the ramp bulbs and stems. Let cool completely. Cover and store in the refrigerator overnight or for up to 2 weeks.

To make the fried rice, whisk the egg with a pinch of salt in a small bowl. Heat 1 table-spoon of the peanut oil over medium-high heat in a large, flat-bottomed wok until shimmery. Add the egg to the wok, stirring for just a few seconds, then swirl the wok so the egg coats the bottom and cook until it's set. Turn

off the heat, scoop out the egg, and chop it into small pieces. Wipe the wok clean.

In a small bowl, combine ½ cup of the liquid from the pickled ramps, the soy sauce, and the mirin and set aside. Heat the remaining 3 tablespoons of peanut oil in the wok over high heat until shimmery. Working quickly, add the ginger and garlic and cook, stirring constantly, for 10 seconds. Add the ham, ramp greens, and fried chicken, and cook, tossing, for 30 seconds. Add the cooked rice, break up any clumps, and toss to coat the rice with the oil. Add the peas, the sliced ramp greens, and the chopped egg and toss until the rice is hot, about 2 minutes. Add the pickling liquid mixture, tossing to incorporate. Season the rice with salt and sprinkle with the peanuts.

W.P. Gold Burger

TOKYO, JAPAN

There is only one place in Tokyo, if not in the whole world, where you can eat burgers named after American actors and actresses whose names lend themselves, vaguely, to beefed-up puns. The Kevin Bacon Burger, at least, comes with bacon, though it's unclear why the Steven Soder Burger is topped with chili (unless we missed a plot point in *Out of Sight*), why the Charlotte Gains Burger comes with three patties when its namesake is notably waifish, or why the mashed potatoes that you can choose instead of fries earn the moniker Natalie Potato-man. Doesn't mean we won't order them, though. They're so good that we'd happily take a meal away from ramen or yakitori for a taste.

The creators are Taiji Kushima and Shogo Kamishima, friends from elementary school and skate punks who stumbled into the burger life. As the two friends tell it, they happened to take the same design class and worked together on an assignment: make flyers for an original business. Loving burgers, as one does, they decided to go with a burger joint. They named it W.P. Gold Burger, Shogo explains, because it was funny. (Get it, like Whoopi Goldberg!) The idea was so good they decided to actually open the place.

The place certainly looks like a restaurant started on a whim. It's located in Shibuya, the neighborhood famous for bright lights (like Times Square times ten), tall malls, and an intersection busier than a newly opened Whole Foods. W.P. Gold Burger, on the other hand, is tiny. On a side street and in a room that's best described as teenager's-basement chic, Tokyo's young burger cognoscenti sit on stools pulled up to the bar, drinking craft beer (pineapple ale from Kanagawa prefecture, maybe) and digging into thoughtfully constructed creations with great bones: idyllic sesame seed buns sandwiching thin patties made from beef that's ground in-house and expertly browned on a mini charcoal grill.

TAIJI KUSHIMA AND SHOGO KAMISHIMA

Puns and buns fell by the wayside when Kushima and Kamishima got to cooking for after-hours. They used that charcoal grill to make the comfort food specialty of their hometown of Obihiro, on the island of Hokkaido, where they met as kids: thinly sliced pork, dunked in a sticky-sweet sauce of soy, sake, and sugar, and served over steaming rice. Even when they ran out of pork loin and had to switch to bacon, the dish still bowled us over.

Sake and Soy–Marinated Pork over Rice   SERVES 4

6 tablespoons soy sauce

3 tablespoons mirin

3 tablespoons sake

3 tablespoons sugar

1 pound boneless pork loin, sliced about ⅛ inch thick (beg your butcher to do this)

Kosher salt and freshly ground black pepper

6 cups steamed short-grain white rice, hot

Thinly sliced scallions, for garnish

In a medium saucepan, combine the soy sauce, mirin, sake, sugar, and 3 tablespoons water and stir well. Bring to a boil, then reduce the heat and simmer until the sugar has dissolved, about 30 seconds. Set aside about ⅓ cup for serving.

Heat a grill or a grill pan over high heat. Lightly season the pork slices on both sides with salt and pepper. When the grill is hot, cook the pork in batches, flipping once and brushing with the sauce, until seared on both sides, about 2 minutes.

Divide the rice among bowls. Top each with a few slices of pork and a sprinkle of scallions. Drizzle with the reserved sauce and serve immediately.

Talde

BROOKLYN, NEW YORK

It's not every day that love blossoms on food TV. But once upon a time, under the bright lights of a *Top Chef* shoot, Dale met Gail.

Don't get us wrong, Gail Simmons and Dale Talde are both happily married and not to each other. But they're total friends forever, even though their relationship began on opposite sides of the judges' table. She is the show's most loveable judge. He was one of our favorite contestants—see: angry outbursts, rapper-level arrogance, underlying teddy bear–like sweetness—then became the chef behind some of our favorite restaurants, where he fuses his French training, Filipino palate, and undying love for Fat Boy cuisine exemplified by McDonald's and Pizza Hut. In other words, Dale and Gail are the two people on the show you actually want to have drinks and snacks with, and so we did.

In his episode, Dale stuck to Brooklyn, eating farm-to-Flatbush Avenue Southern Italian food at Franny's, the kind of food that's so good, it makes you think, "What have I done with my life?" By the time he left Pearl's Social

& Billy Club, so deep into Bushwick that you see "mad handlebar mustaches," you could tell by the glazed look on his face that he really shouldn't have been cooking that night. Lucky for us, we caught him again when he was relatively sober. Gail chose Dale's restaurant Talde, in Park Slope, Brooklyn, as her last stop and, rather adorably, they cooked together. Dale helped her riff on some of her favorites dishes from her travels to Vietnam, Malaysia, and Indonesia, including this killer *nasi goreng-nasi lemak* mash up. As you'd expect, the chef who plunks fried oysters on pad thai and invented buttered-toast ramen isn't a strict traditionalist, so he made nasi goreng (essentially, fried rice made with funky shrimp paste) and served in the style of nasi lemak, a dish of coconut rice surrounded by tasty stuff like peanuts, cucumber, boiled eggs, and tiny, awesomely chewy anchovies. The two pals heaped the rice on a platter and set out little bowls of *accoutrement* for self-service. Gail likened it to a make-your-own-sundae bar. Dale drizzled on tamarind and bacon caramel, as thick as hot fudge. No wonder they like each other.

**BACON-TAMARIND
CARAMEL**

4 ounces bacon, chopped

½ cup granulated sugar

¼ cup unsweetened
coconut milk

½ cup tamarind paste

¼ cup fish sauce

Freshly squeezed juice
of 1 lime

FRIED RICE

¼ cup vegetable oil

6 large eggs, beaten

4 garlic cloves,
thinly sliced

1 medium yellow
onion, diced

6 cups cooked
white rice, at room
temperature

6 tablespoons jarred
ginisang bagoong (sautéed
shrimp paste), preferably
Barrio Fiesta brand

FOR SERVING

¼ cup dried anchovies
(from your Asian grocery)

6 large eggs, soft-cooked
or hard-cooked (whichever
you prefer)

½ cup roasted peanuts,
roughly chopped

1 cucumber, halved and
sliced ¼ inch thick

½ cup roughly chopped
fresh cilantro

½ cup fresh Thai
basil leaves

Nasi Lemak   SERVES 6

To make the bacon-tamarind caramel, line a
plate with paper towels. Cook the bacon in
a medium skillet over medium heat, stirring
occasionally, until it is crispy and the fat has
rendered, about 6 minutes. Using a slotted
spoon, transfer the bacon to the prepared
plate. Add the sugar to the skillet and cook
until golden and caramelized, about 2 minutes. Add the coconut milk and simmer for
5 minutes longer, until thick. Remove from
the heat and stir in the reserved bacon, the
tamarind paste, fish sauce, and lime juice.

To make the fried rice, heat the oil in a large
cast-iron skillet over high heat. Add the eggs
and cook, stirring constantly, until almost set,
about 45 seconds. Add the garlic and onion
and cook until golden brown, about 5 minutes. Add the rice and cook, stirring once in
a while so the rice has a chance to get brown
and crunchy on the bottom, 6 to 8 minutes.
Stir in the shrimp paste.

To serve, heat a small skillet over medium-
high. Add the anchovies and cook, stirring
occasionally, until toasted, about 3 minutes.
Transfer to a plate and let cool. Peel the eggs
and slice them in half lengthwise.

Mound fried rice in the center of 6 plates.
Divide the eggs among the plates, along with
the peanuts, anchovies, cucumber, cilantro,
and basil. Drizzle the rice with the caramel
and serve immediately.

Coi

SAN FRANCISCO, CALIFORNIA

The YouTube comments on Daniel Patterson's night out are some of the most interesting we've ever gotten.

What the fuck did I just watch?

MUNCHIES, don't ever do this bullshit again.

smh

Patterson sparked a level of outrage heretofore unseen in *Chef's Night Out* history. It didn't help that the cerebral genius behind the groundbreaking Coi restaurant in San Francisco is thoughtful to a fault, treating our camera to extemporaneous musings on the bell curve of seasonality, the role of technique in creativity, and eating as an ineffable transfer of energy. This earned him plenty of hate for being a "pretentious asshole," as one of the more temperate trolls put it.

His greatest offense, however, came when he decided that this was a good opportunity for a date night with his wife at Benu. His subdued-evening-with-bae idea ran so counter to the MUNCHIES program that Benu's wunderkind chef Corey Lee openly wondered why they were here sipping Yves Cuilleron Marsanne and cooing over homemade tofu with pickled burdock and not somewhere much less classy getting much more faded.

But count us as fans of Patterson. The man is unapologetically himself, so rather than trying to out-bro or out-drink, he did things his own way. He's the same in real life. Last we checked, rather than just talk shit online, he decided to step down from Coi to focus on LocoL, the fast-food chain he launched, along with certified cool guy Roy Choi, that will ultimately make the world a better place. So, yeah, when his friends joined him for his late-night meal, he didn't make pigtail tacos or deep-fried pizza. He cooked bulgur, mixed it with dandelion green salsa verde, and topped it with griddled veggies and fried eggs. (It is by far the healthiest dish in this book.) Everyone ate it quietly and awkwardly. And it tasted damn good. Do you, chef. Do you.

DANIEL PATTERSON

1 cup bulgur wheat

Kosher salt and freshly
ground black pepper

1 bunch broccolini,
trimmed and cut into
1-inch pieces

2 tablespoons olive oil

2 baby bok choy, thinly
sliced

¼ head green cabbage,
cored and thinly sliced

Dandelion Salsa Verde
(recipe follows)

4 fried eggs, for serving

Hot sauce, for serving

Sautéed Vegetables with Bulgur and Dandelion Salsa Verde *

SERVES 4

the only real vegetable dish in the book

Bring 2 cups water to a boil in a medium saucepan. Add the bulgur and a large pinch of salt and cook until the water is absorbed and the bulgur is tender, about 20 minutes. Spread the bulgur out on a baking sheet to cool slightly.

Bring a large pot of generously salted water to a boil. Set up a big bowl of icy water. Add the broccolini to the boiling water and cook until bright green, 1 to 2 minutes. Drain the broccolini, transfer to the ice water, stir well, then drain again.

Heat the olive oil in a large skillet over medium-high heat. Add the broccolini, bok choy, and cabbage and cook, stirring often, until lightly browned and tender, about 10 minutes. Season with salt and pepper and keep warm.

To serve, mix the bulgur with dandelion salsa verde to taste, then spoon into individual bowls. Top with the vegetables and a fried egg. Shake your favorite hot sauce over everything.

Dandelion Salsa Verde MAKES ½ CUP

1 medium shallot, minced

4 teaspoons champagne vinegar, plus more if needed

Kosher salt

1 bunch dandelion greens, bottom 1 inch trimmed

¼ cup good extra-virgin olive oil

2 tablespoons drained capers, minced

Finely grated zest of 1 lemon

2 tablespoons freshly squeezed lemon juice, plus more if needed

Combine the shallots, vinegar, and a pinch of salt in a medium bowl, stir well, and let the mixture sit for 20 minutes. Meanwhile, bring a large pot of generously salted water to a boil. Add the dandelion greens and cook until tender, about 2 minutes. Drain the greens and run under cold water until cooled. Squeeze the moisture from the greens and chop them finely.

Add the oil, capers, lemon zest, lemon juice, and chopped dandelion greens to the bowl with the shallots and stir really well. Season with salt, then add more lemon or vinegar so it tastes bright. Use right away or store in an airtight container in the fridge for up to 3 days.

CHAPTER 6

Meat and Seafood

Charlie Bird

NEW YORK, NEW YORK

When the dean of law school tells you to quit memorizing statutes and start drinking more wine, you listen. Robert Bohr sure did, dropping out of NYU to sling Burgundy and Brunello for New York's finest chefs, from Batali to Boulud. We started hearing his name back when he was presiding over the three-thousand-wines-strong list at Cru, where the selection required a Wall Street wine collector to assemble it, two leatherbound volumes to catalog it, and a friend with a job at Lehman Brothers to sample it. Now Bohr is finally living the dream: Ninety-nine percent of chefs want to run a restaurant where they'd go to eat, so Bohr went in on Charlie Bird, a place where he'd go to drink and eat impeccable Italian food, and Pasquale Jones, a place where he'd go to drink and eat impeccable pizza.

Tagging along with Bohr taught us something: Life as a well-respected wino doesn't seem so bad. When chefs go out, they get extra plates of mortadella and octopus. When wine people roll into a restaurant, premier cru is dropped on the table like breadsticks at Olive Garden.

He and his sommelier friends straight nerded out, letting loose strings of syllables that will inspire either confusion or jealousy, depending entirely on the depth of your wine knowledge. After so much sour grape juice, including a "sick" 1996 d'Angerville Volnay and a "unicorn wine" (in this case, Côte-Rôtie from Gentaz-Dervieux), they went back to Charlie Bird. Chef Ryan Hardy toiled in the kitchen and Bohr did the sommelier equivalent, uncorking off-the-list bottles and holding forth on their awesomeness. As Hardy fried up some truly excellent buttermilk-and-chile-marinated chicken, then dusted it with fennel pollen, he took a swig of beer.

"RUN DMC APPROVED"

3 pounds bone-in, skin-on chicken breasts, thighs, drumsticks, and wings

4 cups buttermilk

1 tablespoon Aleppo pepper

1 tablespoon fennel seeds, coarsely crushed

1 tablespoon Calabrian chile paste

2 fresh rosemary sprigs, leaves picked

1 head garlic, cloves separated, crushed, and peeled

2 tablespoons freshly ground black pepper

4 tablespoons kosher salt

3 cups all-purpose flour

TO FRY AND SEASON THE CHICKEN

Canola oil, for deep frying

1 tablespoon fennel pollen (optional)

1 tablespoon crushed red pepper flakes

1 teaspoon kosher salt

Lemon wedges, for serving

Tuscan Fried Chicken   SERVES 4

Cut any chicken breasts crosswise into thirds through the bone. Cut any thighs in half through the bone.

In a large bowl, combine the buttermilk, Aleppo pepper, fennel seeds, chile paste, rosemary, garlic, 1 tablespoon of the black pepper, and 3 tablespoons of the salt and stir well. Add the chicken pieces, toss to coat, cover, and marinate in the fridge overnight.

Set a wire rack over a baking sheet and line a second baking sheet with paper towels. In a mixing bowl, combine the flour, the remaining 1 tablespoon black pepper, and the remaining 1 tablespoon salt. One by one, remove the chicken pieces from the buttermilk, toss them in the flour mixture until well coated, then transfer to the wire rack.

Heat 4 inches of oil in a large saucepan until a deep-fry thermometer reaches 350°F. Working in batches of 4 or 5 pieces, fry the chicken, turning the pieces every minute, until golden brown and the internal temperature is 155°F, 8 to 10 minutes. Transfer the chicken pieces to the paper towel–lined baking sheet and immediately sprinkle with some of the fennel pollen, red pepper flakes, and salt.

Serve the chicken warm with lemon wedges.

Bizarre Foods Guru

MINNEAPOLIS, MINNESOTA

Andrew Zimmern has been around. Not just flying around the world, gnawing on innards, chomping on tarantulas, and otherwise grossing out Middle America and, okay, sometimes us, too. (It's a neat trick that exploits our culinary voyeurism to remind us how naïve we really are—after all, one culture's shrimp is another's creepy seabug.) Once upon a time, he was a young alcoholic and heroin addict. Before completely cratering, he worked as a cook at some of the best restaurants in New York City. He did a year at Rakel, which Thomas Keller opened 150 years before The French Laundry, before decamping somewhere around the time Keller found him passed out on the floor of the liquor closet. In Andrew's telling, when Keller bumped into him years later, the chef made a beeline toward him, gave him a hug, and whispered, "I thought you were dead."

We caught The Man Who Ate Muskrat, who it should be noted has been clean for more than twenty-five years, on a visit to New York from his home base in Minneapolis. While the night began with a plate of brains and sweetbreads at Osteria Morini, there was enough pasta on the table to keep things decidedly unbizarre. He stopped by Marc Forgione's eponymous restaurant, reminiscing about the half-day he worked for Marc's dad at the trailblazing An American Place before getting (deservedly) canned. By the end of the evening, Andrew was behind the stove at Barbuto, the restaurant of his friend and culinary pioneer Jonathan Waxman, cooking chicken for the Chicken King. Waxman may be best known for perfecting the roast bird, but Andrew absolutely murdered some chicken, simmering it in soy sauce, sugar, star anise, and cinnamon until the sauce was sticky and clung to it like Zimmern to a particularly tasty beetle.

ANDREW ZIMMERN

3 pounds chicken wings, split, tips removed

2 tablespoons minced ginger

4 dried chiles de árbol

2 whole star anise

1 (3-inch) cinnamon stick

⅓ cup sake

⅓ cup soy sauce

3 tablespoons oyster sauce

3 tablespoons mirin

3 tablespoons sugar

2 scallions, thinly sliced

2 limes, cut into wedges, for serving

One-Pot Sticky Chicken Wings SERVES 6

In a large, dry Dutch oven or nonstick saucepan, cooking in batches if needed, brown the chicken wings on both sides, about 8 minutes total. Reduce the heat to medium-low and add the ginger, chiles, star anise, and cinnamon to the pot. Stir until the ingredients are fragrant, about 1 minute. Add the sake, soy sauce, oyster sauce, mirin, sugar, and ⅓ cup water. Increase the heat and bring to a gentle simmer, then cover the pot and cook for 10 minutes.

Remove the lid, increase the heat to medium-high, and simmer vigorously, stirring and tossing occasionally, until the sauce has reduced to a thick glaze that coats the wings, about 8 minutes.

Transfer the chicken wings to a platter and scatter the scallions on top. Serve the wings with the lime wedges on the side.

Han Dynasty

PHILADELPHIA, PENNSYLVANIA

Han Chiang's cameo sold us. When he showed up during fellow Philadelphian Brad Spence's night out (page 32), we saw a man just on the brink of insanity, where genius often lives. So we eagerly invited our cameras to capture a night with him in charge.

Born in Taiwan, he moved with his family to Amishville, Pennsylvania, when he was thirteen. His first taste of Chinese food in America—a meal featuring homogenized, warped dishes like General Tso's chicken—didn't so much bring the memories rushing back as it did thoroughly piss him off. Later, after he dropped out of college, he decided to open Han Dynasty in Exton, Pennsylvania—smack between Philly and horse-and-buggy country—that served no-holds-barred renditions of the food of Sichuan province, where his dad is from. When he realized that the chef he'd hired was a complete asshole, Han learned to cook himself, enrolling in culinary school in Chengdu.

Through luck, a knack for publicity, and sheer force of will, his risky venture blossomed into a mini-chain that's already extended to Manhattan. And he has fashioned himself as part culinary ambassador, part mapo tofu nazi: The same guy who helpfully created a 1-to-10 heat scale for each dish (to help customers understand what they were in for) is also known for berating them for offenses as egregious as asking for sweet-and-sour chicken. Maybe that's why one woman called the cops on him: She thought her food was not just too spicy—but suspiciously spicy.

As you might expect, Han is drawn to cooks who don't hold back. At the art-cluttered home of Philly-famous mosaic muralist Isaiah Zagar, he and his friends eat *barbacoa* and hand-pressed tortillas cooked by Christina Martinez, whose slow-cooked lamb, served at her cart turned brick-and-mortar in South Philly, has made her a national sensation. Soon after Han takes down a taco topped with salsa and a freshly plucked eyeball, he's hacking off the head of a crisp-skinned suckling pig hauled from the oven by his old pal Spence. They help each other dismember the creature, then pile meat on a surfboard-size pizza—as Spence says, it's Rome meets Philadelphia. And somehow, he's still hungry enough when he makes it to Prime Stache to "want to fuck" the so-big-it's-spherical sandwich piled with pork belly, loin, and shoulder, which he eats with Philadelphia Eagles center and certified gentle giant Jason Kelce. Han has consumed as much booze as he has food, so by the time he's deep-frying chicken wings back at Han Dynasty, he really shouldn't be allowed to operate a wok.

We know saucy wings. Saucy wings are friends of ours. But these are no saucy wings. Instead, they get their flavor power from the Sichuan technique of dry-frying: first the cornstarch-dredged wings are dunked in hot oil, then they take a brief trip in a pan with ginger, garlic, scallions, and a daunting amount of dried chiles. This creates a dry-ish, intensely delicious, just-spicy-enough coating that clings to the super-crisp skin. We highly recommend not skipping the dash of Vitamin M, which is how Chiang refers to good old-fashioned MSG. In case you haven't heard, MSG is magic, not poison. Used with discretion, it makes good things taste even better.

MARINADE

1 cup cooking sherry

1 teaspoon freshly ground white pepper

½ cup cornstarch

1 teaspoon granulated sugar

½ teaspoon cayenne pepper

2 tablespoons minced garlic

2 tablespoons minced ginger

1½ pounds chicken wings

TO FRY AND SEASON THE CHICKEN

Canola oil, for frying

1 cup cornstarch

1 (6-inch) piece ginger, peeled and thinly sliced

2 garlic cloves, thinly sliced

2 scallions, thinly sliced

2 tablespoons Asian chili paste

½ cup dried red Asian chiles

1 pinch MSG

½ teaspoon granulated sugar

Kosher salt

Spicy Chicken Wings   SERVES 4

To make the marinade, combine the sherry, white pepper, cornstarch, sugar, cayenne, garlic, and ginger in a large bowl, and stir well. Add the chicken to the mixture and toss to coat. Cover the bowl with plastic wrap and refrigerate for at least 4 hours or up to overnight.

The next day, heat 4 inches of oil in a large saucepan until a deep-fry thermometer reaches 375°F. Line a baking sheet with paper towels. Remove the chicken from the marinade and toss in a large bowl with the cornstarch until well coated. Working in batches to avoid crowding, fry the chicken until crispy and cooked through, 8 to 10 minutes. As they're done, transfer the wings to the prepared baking sheet.

Heat ½ cup of oil in a large wok over high heat until the oil is good and hot. Add the ginger, garlic, and scallions and stir and toss constantly for a few seconds, just until aromatic. Add the chili paste and dried chiles and cook, stirring constantly, until the chiles brown a bit, about 1 minute, lowering the temperature if necessary to prevent burning. Add the chicken wings and the MSG, sugar, and salt to taste, toss until well coated and heated through, about 2 minutes more. Dump it all on a plate and eat right away.

Hopgood's Foodliner

TORONTO, CANADA

We miss the days when we could go to Toronto's Hopgood's Foodliner and pretend we were in Nova Scotia. Named for Geoff Hopgood's great-grandparents' grocery store in the Maritime provinces, the restaurant might have gone the way of so many great establishments, but that doesn't mean we're ready to let go. The pleasure of eating there wasn't just the impeccable seafood they sourced, but the spirit with which they served it. It was the kind of place where you could rent out the modest back room and feast on an ocean's worth of briny creatures—cracking into snow crabs, tonguing raw clams and still-in-the-shell scallops. When Geoff and his friends—including our dear Matty Matheson (future host of VICELAND's *Dead Set on Life*, seen here with tattooed belly exposed by an unbuttoned Yankees jersey)—gathered there, they showed us how to do it right.

When it comes to building a seafood tower for your party of friends, live like Hopgood's and place everything in the middle of the table: fresh scallops, clams, lobsters, snow crab. They can shuck at their own discretion. . . .

The best seafood needs nothing but a cool ocean breeze, but drawn butter doesn't hurt. Everyone basically disagrees on exactly what it is—is it clarified butter, melted, or something in between?—but we'll take ours simply liquefied over gentle heat, then, as Hopgood did, kept warm over a candle at the table. Appropriate dippables include steamed lobster, crab, and shrimp.

Sure, serve raw oysters with mignonette (the "recipe" is red wine vinegar, finely chopped shallots, and black pepper). But do like Hopgood's and scoop on jiggly roasted bone marrow. Just roast bones, halved lengthwise by your butcher and generously seasoned with salt by you, at about 450°F for, oh, 25 minutes or so. The marrow should be very soft but not so liquidy it oozes onto the pan.

Set out these crab legs (page 166) from fellow Torontonian chef Grant van Gameren, who serves them on the "big gangster platters" he brings out to late-night stragglers at Bar Isabel.

Add surf to your turf: Van Gameren likes to sneak fried chicken and a seasoned and simply seared lobe of foie gras onto his platters. May we recommend the exceptionally crunchy poultry from Charlie Bird (page 155)?

Save the empty shells from lobster tails—not for stock, but for the classy-trashy party accessory known as the lobster luge. Hold the wide end to your mouth, pour in liquor of choice, repeat. Pro tip: Marrow bones work, too.

A grandmother's ragu. A father's diner. Lamb roasted over fire. Chefs cite many reasons that inspired a life in the kitchen. But the path to a life behind the stove isn't always romantic. Take Grant van Gameren, who came to cooking for the reasons many young cooks do, to support a habit: in his case, a fifty-strong collection of snakes. At some point, though, the same obsessive nature that had him breeding blood pythons transferred to making charcuterie and marinating anchovies. Now van Gameren runs Bar Raval and Bar Isabel, where octopus is grilled and served whole, the late-night menu gets weird (in a good way), and sherry-sipping diners get messy cracking into these ridiculously good, ridiculously large king crab legs doused with garlic, ginger, and paprika and sauced with emulsified buttery, crabby goodness.

1 pound frozen Alaskan king crab legs	2 tablespoons minced ginger	1 teaspoon crushed red pepper flakes (optional)	2 tablespoons chopped fresh flat-leaf parsley
¼ cup olive oil, plus a splash	1 tablespoon smoked paprika	Freshly squeezed juice of 1 lemon	Crusty bread, for serving
2 tablespoons minced garlic	2 tablespoons unsalted butter	Kosher salt	

Butter-Basted Crab Legs with Garlic, Ginger, and Chili SERVES 2

With the crab legs still frozen, take a heavy, sharp knife and hack at the legs at a 20-degree angle, chipping away just enough of the shell to make small pockets of exposed flesh every few inches. This is for maximum flavor penetration. Thaw the crab legs in the refrigerator overnight in a covered bowl. Reserve the liquid they release.

Mix the ¼ cup olive oil, garlic, ginger, and paprika together in a small bowl. Use a pastry brush or your hands to massage this mixture into the crevices of the crab legs. Marinate the crab for several hours in the fridge; the longer the better.

Heat the oven to 400°F. Put the crab in a large ovenproof skillet. If the legs are too big to fit in the pan, break them in half. Roast until they're warmed through (frozen crab

legs have already been cooked, so you're just reheating them), about 5 minutes.

Transfer the pan from the oven to a burner set at medium heat. Add the butter and a splash of olive oil. Use a spoon to baste the crab legs all over and in all their crevices. After a few minutes, when you can smell the toasted garlic and ginger, add the red pepper flakes (if you like it spicy), then the reserved crab liquid and the lemon juice. Keep basting until you have a nice emulsification of buttery, crabby goodness in the bottom of the pan, about 5 minutes.

Season with salt to taste. Off the heat, add the parsley, toss well, and scrape the crab legs onto a plate with all the juices. Serve with bread and a few sets of crab crackers to break into the crab.

If Phet Schwader can get people in TriBeCa, the $5-million-loft capital of the world, to eat with their hands, he can do anything. Born in Laos and raised in Wichita, Schwader grew up eating Laotian food cooked by his mother and other members of the small but strong community of refugees who settled there. Aside from the occasional KFC run, his childhood was fueled almost exclusively by mounds of sticky rice to eat with slivers of sun-dried beef, papaya salad, and dip made from tomatoes, chiles, and *padek*, a fermented fish sludge with the umami of the more familiar filtered fish sauce but with a more racy, exhilarating funk.

Now Schwader serves food inspired by, though not wedded to, the flavors of Laos: crispy pig face with herbs, plus sauces, salads, and curries made with generous doses of *padek*, which in his kitchen goes by "the funk."

Because New York isn't Wichita, let alone Vientiane, his food isn't always easy to make, though it helps that his uncle ships him homemade sun-dried fish. So when he shared his late-night dish with us, he kept Laos out of the picture, choosing a super doable dish of hacked-up crab in a beer- and butter-spiked garlicky black bean sauce. It's a little Chinese, a little French, and thoroughly Schwader. Toasts, slathered with Sriracha mayo if you get down like that, are necessary for soaking up the soupy sauce. But to get at that sweet, sweet crab, you'll have to get in there with your hands.

Beer and Butter–Spiked Crab in Black Bean Sauce   SERVES 8

2 tablespoons canola oil

1 cup julienned ginger

4 Dungeness crabs, 1½ to 2 pounds each, legs, claws, and bodies separated (ask your fishmonger to do this)

2 medium yellow onions, thinly sliced

½ cup black bean garlic sauce

5 tablespoons granulated sugar

1 cup oyster sauce

Two dashes fish sauce, preferably Three Crabs brand, plus more as needed

6 (11.5-ounce) bottles Beer Lao or light beer of your choice

1 cup fresh Thai basil leaves

1 cup (2 sticks) unsalted butter, cubed

1 loaf of bread, preferably light and crusty, cut into thick slices

Sriracha, for serving

Mayonnaise, preferably Kewpie, for serving

Heat the canola oil in a large saucepan over medium-high. Add the ginger and cook, stirring, until golden-brown, about 2 minutes. Add the crabs, onions, black bean garlic sauce, sugar, oyster sauce, and a couple of dashes of fish sauce and stir really well. Add the beer, let it come to a simmer, and cook until the liquid has reduced by a quarter, about 5 minutes. Season to taste with more fish sauce. Stir in the Thai basil and butter.

Lightly toast the bread. Top each slice with a drizzle of Sriracha and plenty of mayonnaise. Serve the crab in the pot with a serving spoon and the bread on the side for dipping.

Mission Chinese Food

NEW YORK, NEW YORK

Danny Bowien's path to food-world royalty was as typical as his signature kung pao pastrami is authentic. Adopted from Korea and raised super-religious in Oklahoma City (where, as you might expect, a tornado blew away his high school), he did a stint in a Christian rock band (which, fun fact, once opened for the Flaming Lips) before finding his home in the kitchen. He cooked around San Francisco, then did something weird, and we don't mean winning the World Pesto Championship, which also happened. He started a restaurant. Inside of another restaurant. While that restaurant was still operating. The San Francisco Chinese restaurant Lung Shan in the Mission agreed to share its kitchen, churning out lo mein while Bowien made Chongqing chicken wings. He rode the wave of acclaim that followed, eventually opening a location in New York that was equally odd and wonderful—the *Twin Peaks*–inspired bathroom, the keg on the floor, the precarious space that was almost destined to get shut down, and ultimately was. Now in sturdier digs in Chinatown, he continues practicing his brand of remixed Sichuan-influenced food that has no allegiance to anything but flavor.

We caught his antics on camera way back when he was only a local sensation. But it speaks to the food industry's love and respect for Bowien in that he has appeared in a good four or so episodes since. He is the man in the striped shirt (or really, in the short shorts) in the Where's Waldo of *Chef's Night Out*.

We do not recommend cleaning and dismembering live crabs while under the influence, as Bowien and friends did—more or less successfully—back in the kitchen at the OG Mission Chinese Food in San Francisco. But we can endorse with confidence making Cantonese-ish salt-and-pepper crab, then dousing the result with a sauce packed with the lip-tingling flavors of the Sichuan classic mapo tofu. Like just about all of Bowien's food, it's never been done before, but is so good it's destined to be done again and again.

Salt-and-Pepper Crab with Mapo Tofu   SERVES 6

MAPO TOFU BASE

2 ounces dried whole shiitake mushrooms

⅓ cup soy sauce

½ cup doubanjiang (spicy bean paste)

⅓ cup tomato paste

MAPO TOFU BRAISE

½ cup chili oil, plus more if needed

15 garlic cloves, minced

¼ cup fermented black beans

⅓ cup chili crisp sauce, preferably Laoganma brand

½ pound ground pork

1 (12-ounce) bottle cheap beer

½ teaspoon fish sauce

2 teaspoons mushroom powder

1 teaspoon toasted and ground Sichuan peppercorns

1 (15-ounce) package firm tofu, cut into 1-inch cubes

1 teaspoon cornstarch mixed with 1 teaspoon of water (optional)

Soy sauce, as needed

1 or 2 scallions, sliced

SALT AND PEPPER CRAB

1 live Dungeness crab, legs, claws, and bodies separated (ask your fishmonger to do this, or see the instructions on page 172)

Kosher salt and freshly ground white pepper

Canola oil, for frying

½ cup all-purpose flour

½ cup cornstarch

½ yellow onion, thinly sliced

1 jalapeño, cut into thin rounds

2 teaspoons granulated sugar

TO SERVE

1 tablespoon chili oil

2 tablespoons fried shallots

3 tablespoons fried garlic

½ cup fresh cilantro leaves

2 teaspoons toasted and ground Sichuan peppercorns

To make the base, in a medium bowl, cover the shiitake mushrooms with 3 cups of boiling water. Add the soy sauce and allow the mushrooms to soak for at least an hour, or until completely rehydrated and soft.

Drain the mushrooms and reserve the liquid. In a food processor, pulse the mushrooms into small chunks. You should have about 1 cup of chopped mushrooms.

Combine the reserved mushroom liquid, doubanjiang, and tomato paste in a medium bowl. Whisk to combine, then add the chopped mushrooms. You will have about 3½ cups of the base; set 2 cups aside and transfer the rest to an airtight container and refrigerate for later.

To make the mapo tofu braise, in a large saucepan, heat the chili oil over medium heat. Add the garlic, fermented black beans, and chili crisp sauce and cook, stirring occasionally, until the garlic softens and the mixture becomes spine-tinglingly aromatic, 2 to 3 minutes. Using a slotted spoon, scoop the solids out of the oil as best you can and set them aside in a bowl.

Increase the heat to high and get the chili oil almost smoking hot. Add the pork to the pan and cook, using a spoon to break up the meat, until thoroughly browned, 5 to 7 minutes.

When you've got good color on the meat, add the beer. Scrape up all the crispy bits from the bottom of the pan and stir well. Add the reserved solids back to the pan, along with the fish sauce, mushroom powder, Sichuan pepper, and the 2 cups mapo tofu base and bring to a simmer. The sauce should look like thin marinara sauce; if it's too thick, thin it with more base. Cover and simmer over low heat for 2 hours.

Bring a pot of well-salted water to a boil. Cook the tofu cubes for 1 minute, then drain carefully so they don't break up too much and set aside.

If you want a thicker sauce, stir in the cornstarch-water slurry and bring to a simmer. Once the sauce thickens, fold in the tofu and slowly warm it through. Taste and season with soy sauce as needed. There should be a thin puddle of shiny red oil on top of the sauce—if not, add a few more tablespoons of chili oil. Stir in the scallions and keep the mapo tofu warm while you prepare the crab.

Tap on each crab leg with the back of the cleaver to crack it for easier eating. Season all the pieces liberally with salt and white pepper.

In a large saucepan, heat about 3 inches of canola oil to 350°F. Set a rack over a baking sheet. Meanwhile, mix together the flour and cornstarch in a large shallow bowl. Coat each piece of crab, including the top shell and guts, with the flour mixture and tap off any excess.

Working in batches, add the crab pieces to the hot oil; fry the top shell last. Fry, moving them around so they cook evenly, until golden brown, about 2 minutes. Transfer the finished pieces to the rack. When removing the top shell from the oil, take care to drain the oil from inside the shell before transferring it to the rack.

Set a large wok or skillet over high heat and let it sit for a minute, until it gets very hot. Slick the pan with a couple of tablespoons of the frying oil, then add the onion and cook for 1 minute. Give the pan a few shakes and let the onion get a nice sear, then add the jalapeño and cook for 1 minute more. Add the fried crab, season everything with more salt and white pepper and the sugar, and toss a couple times to combine.

Transfer the crab to a platter and smother it with the mapo tofu. Drizzle with the chili oil and sprinkle with the fried shallots, fried garlic, and cilantro. Sprinkle on the Sichuan pepper and serve immediately.

BUTCHERING DUNGENESS CRABS

To humanely kill a Dungeness crab at home, first sedate the crab by putting it in the freezer for 15 to 30 minutes.

Next, place the crab belly-up on a cutting board. Working quickly, pry open the triangular flap, steady the tip of a sturdy knife, ice pick, or clean screwdriver at the tip of the opening, and use both hands to firmly push down on the knife. Locate the indentation on the front of the crab and on a slight angle, steady the tip of the knife in the indentation and with force, insert the tip an inch or two into the crab.

Pry off the top shell and set it aside, shell side down to preserve the tasty guts. Pull off the gills and discard them. Break the body in half lengthwise, using brute strength or a cleaver. Chop each half between the legs into three pieces.

The success of a restaurant like Michael's Genuine seems obvious in retrospect. *Of course* it made sense to deviate from the clubby, Asian lettuce wrap–fueled lounges of South Beach and open a neighborhood joint in an area optimistically called the Design District, way back before it was packed with Gucci boutiques. Today the neighborhood is bumping, and the namesake chef, Michael Schwartz, has a small empire of restaurants dedicated to cooking that celebrates the bounty of South Florida. His food drove the scene, not the other way around. Eating in Miami hasn't been the same since.

For Schwartz, perhaps the most exciting part of that bounty comes from the sea—from the boiled stone crabs he rocks with green sambal, to the tilefish he roasts in the wood oven, to the spiny lobster he turns into ceviche. The magic of briefly marinated seafood is especially useful for the tipsy snacker, because it's the epitome of low-effort cookery. Once you mix citrus, rice vinegar, and soy sauce in Schwartz's prescribed proportions to maximize tangy, salty exhilaration, you use it to marinate the flesh of an exceedingly fresh creature for half an hour, technically cooking it but maintaining its raw vibe. The crunch of cucumber, the heat of jalapeño, and the snap of briny, diminutive fish eggs makes a good thing even better.

And sure, if you can't find the clawless crustacean caught in warm Florida waters, sub in uncooked Maine lobster tail, scallops, shrimp, or sea bass for an equally wondrous result.

Miami-Style Ceviche   SERVES 2

½ cup soy sauce

⅓ cup freshly squeezed lemon juice, plus more if needed

2½ tablespoons freshly squeezed lime juice, plus more if needed

2 tablespoons rice vinegar

Pinch of cayenne pepper

4 ounces spiny lobster tail meat, thinly sliced

1 small seedless cucumber, thinly sliced

1 tablespoon fresh masago or tobiko

½ jalapeño, thinly sliced

Combine the soy sauce, lemon and lime juices, vinegar, and cayenne in a medium mixing bowl.

Add the lobster meat and make sure it is completely submerged in the liquid. Let the lobster soak for 30 minutes.

Taste and add more lemon or lime juice if you want.

Serve the lobster ceviche with the cucumbers, topped with the masago and jalapeño.

You've never heard anybody wax more lyrical about the espresso martini, or the value of mayonnaise in sushi, than Konstantin Filippou did on his night out with us. Which is not quite what you'd expect from a fancy, heralded chef. But then again, neither is smashing wineglasses to bits on the street.

But Filippou is kind of a bomb-thrower anyway, so it makes sense. His namesake restaurant amounts to an exquisitely crafted Molotov cocktail chucked into the staid fine-dining traditions of Vienna. Instead of riffing on *knodel* and *schnitzel*, he trains his wide-ranging palate and avant-garde outlook on the continent's finest ingredients and goes wild.

Bless his heart, the half Greek, half Austrian (he was born in Styria) did not subject his tipsy friends to aerated brandade with caviar; instead, he gave them super-satisfying saganaki. The word *saganaki* refers to a two-handled pan that cooks use to cook said dairy product but also other stuff, like this dish, modeled on one that Filippou's grandmother used to make. It's a dead-simple tomatoey shrimp stew—with cheese.

Shrimp stock is easy: simply simmer the shells in plain old water for 20 minutes. Do it and strain it, or just use store-bought stock.

Shrimp Saganaki with Feta and Tomatoes   SERVES 4

5 tablespoons olive oil

2 garlic cloves, minced

1 small yellow onion, diced

2 (28-ounce) cans whole peeled tomatoes, crushed by hand

4 tablespoons unsalted butter

2 tablespoons granulated sugar

Kosher salt and freshly ground black pepper

2 pounds medium shrimp, peeled and deveined

1 pound feta cheese, cut into 1-inch cubes

½ cup shrimp or seafood stock

Fresh flat-leaf parsley leaves, for garnish

Heat 2 tablespoons of the olive oil in a medium saucepan over medium-high. Add the garlic and onion and cook, stirring occasionally, until soft, about 2 minutes. Add the tomatoes, butter, and sugar, season with salt and pepper, and cook, stirring occasionally, until thick, 15 to 17 minutes. Transfer to a blender and puree until smooth. Return the sauce to the saucepan and keep warm.

Meanwhile, heat a grill. Toss the shrimp with the remaining 3 tablespoons olive oil, season with salt and pepper, and cook, flipping once, until cooked through, 4 minutes.

Add the shrimp and feta to the tomato sauce, along with the shrimp stock. Season with salt and pepper and spoon into bowls. Garnish with parsley leaves and serve right away.

Maaemo

OSLO, NORWAY

Asked to name their current favorite ingredient, most trailblazers of the new Nordic cuisine typically choose something alien—reindeer heart, perhaps, or foraged sloe berries. But Esben Holmboe Bang, suffering from the sort of ardent drinking that happens when someone else foots the bill, selected a more familiar item: aspirin. The evening before had been a rough one for the chef of Maaemo, in Oslo, just five minutes from the city's main train station and twice that from the brackish waters and mist-shrouded forests that inspire dishes like scallop mousseline with sea buckthorn berries and an intricate dessert celebrating the black currant, including a sorbet made from the stems and leaves of the bush on which the fruit grows. All for the low, low price of $350 a head.

Bang's food might be firmly tied to place, but when we went out with him, he started with shots of Fernet-Branca and moved on to mezcal and tacos before finally coming home to *løyrom* (whitefish roe) at his buddy's restaurant, Arakataka, and *skåling* with aquavit at the bar No. 19. (As much as we love the Scandinavian spirit, we'll take ours in Maaemo's Midnight Sun cocktail, page 9, rather than straight up.) As the night wound down, the chef, his staff, and his friends gathered in his restaurant's gleaming kitchen for a meal meant to soak up all that booze: the stewed ribs of salted sheep and steamed cabbage slicked with the animal's fat. Slurring slightly, the Michelin-starred descendant of Vikings discouraged the use of utensils. "We were good at robbing, raping, and eating with our hands," he said. "Tonight we're only going to eat with our hands."

When Esben agreed to share his recipe for salted sheep ribs, we inquired whether cooks eager to experience the pleasures of ridiculously tender meat sauced with, more or less, its own concentrated juices could get away with substituting pork ribs, because they're a bit easier to find at your local grocery store. He looked at us like a French chef who'd just been asked if beef bourguignon could be made with tofu. So find a good butcher who will sell you mutton (from an adult sheep), hogget (the sheep equivalent of a teen), or even lamb (a young beast) ribs, which offer decreasing degrees of musty funk. It'll make you feel like you're hanging out in Norway but, you know, without the whole freezing to death thing. Or use pork and keep the swap to yourself.

1 (2¾- to 3-pound) rack of sheep, mutton, or pork spareribs, trimmed of large pieces of fat (reserve the fat)

½ cup kosher salt

2 cups lamb or pork stock

Pork lard, as needed

1 large head green cabbage, cored and cut into 1-inch pieces

1 cup porter or stout

Good-quality sea salt

5 tablespoons salted butter, softened

Salted Ribs with Braised Cabbage   SERVES 4 TO 6

Place the rack of ribs on a rimmed baking sheet, then rub all over with the salt. Cover loosely with a damp kitchen towel and refrigerate for 2 days, turning once halfway through. Heat the oven to 200°F. Rinse the salt off the ribs, then place the rack in a large roasting pan. Pour the stock into the pan, cover with foil, and bake until the ribs are tender but not falling easily off the bone, 3 to 4 hours.

Meanwhile, place all the bits of fat trimmed from the ribs in a small saucepan with about ½ cup water. Place the pan over medium-low heat and simmer until all the water has cooked off and the solids begin to brown and sizzle in the fat. Remove the pan from the heat, pour the fat through a fine sieve set over a small heatproof bowl, and discard the solids. Measure ½ cup of the rendered fat and discard the rest. If you don't have enough fat, add pork lard to make ½ cup, or use all pork lard.

When the ribs come out of the oven, set them aside and make the cabbage. Melt the sheep fat in a large cast-iron skillet over medium-high heat. Add the cabbage, cover, and cook, stirring occasionally, until tender and caramelized, 12 to 15 minutes. Add the beer and cook, stirring, until syrupy and almost completely evaporated, about 4 minutes. Remove the pan from the heat. Season to taste with salt and keep warm.

Uncover the ribs and transfer them to a serving platter. Pour the liquid remaining in the roasting pan through a sieve into a small saucepan, bring to a boil over high heat, and cook until reduced by two-thirds, about 3 minutes. Remove the pan from the heat and add the butter a little at a time, swirling constantly, until the sauce is smooth. Spoon the sauce over the ribs and serve everything warm. Eat with your hands.

State Bird Provisions

SAN FRANCISCO, CALIFORNIA

The husband-and-wife team behind State Bird Provisions (and the adjoining The Progress) has won all the awards. In 2012, they turned a derelict spot not just far from the boutiques, Bi-Rites, and restaurants with ampersands in their names but also in an up-and-coming neighborhood that doesn't even have a cute acronym yet. Still, every night a line forms an hour before they open, all because Stuart Brioza and Nicole Krasinski took a wacky idea and made it into a genius one.

The two once helmed the fancy-wino-paradise Rubicon, but when it closed, they decided to go all in on an idea they'd had years before on an airplane, one so good they scribbled it down on a barf bag. They'd serve their food dim sum style. Today, about half of Brioza's food isn't printed on the menu but confronts you on carts, where it's even harder to resist. Before you've had a chance to order the justly famous seed-crusted fried quail with Parm and sweet-and-sour onions or an array of savory pancakes topped with raw sea urchin or sliced beef tongue, you're staring down salmon tartare with fermented turnips, financiers with duck liver mousse, and raw oysters topped with kohlrabi kraut. By the time you try Krasinski's mind-bending ice cream sandwiches or her stroke-of-genius mini dessert—a shot of chilled, sweet peanut milk—you're all, *What the fuck just happened?* Then: *Can I do it again?*

When you come home from boozing, you want food, but you don't necessarily want to cook it, nor should you be allowed near fire. Brioza gets it. He put his Malaysian-inspired oxtail curry—lots of ingredients, easy to pull together—in the oven before he'd had his first adult beverage. When he returned, sloshed, to State Bird—rumor had it he'd get cuddly, and he certainly gave out a lot of hugs—he was coordinated just enough to haul the pot onto the counter of the restaurant's open kitchen without incident. His better half, who was also better behaved, whipped up ridiculously buttery roti, which only the best among you will opt to make and not buy frozen at Asian supermarkets, where it's sold as roti canai or roti paratha.

Oxtail Curry with Roti   SERVES 8 TO 10

5 pounds oxtails

Kosher salt and freshly ground black pepper

¾ cup curry powder

2¼ teaspoons wet shrimp paste

1½ teaspoons ground cardamom

6 cloves garlic, peeled and smashed flat

5 whole star anise

5 whole cloves

2 makrut lime leaves

2 red bell peppers, stemmed, seeded, and roughly chopped

1½ stalks lemongrass, smashed with the flat of a knife blade and cut into large chunks

1 cinnamon stick

1 sprig curry leaves

1 large yellow onion, thinly sliced

1 (3-inch) piece ginger, peeled and thinly sliced

1½ pounds tomatoes, cored and quartered

2 (13.5-ounce) cans unsweetened coconut milk

Freshly squeezed lime juice, to taste

Fish sauce, to taste

FOR SERVING

Chopped fresh cilantro

Chopped fresh mint

Lime wedges

Roti (page 184)

Heat the oven to 400°F. Place the oxtails in a very large, deep flameproof roasting pan, season liberally with salt and pepper, and roast until golden brown, 45 minutes to 1 hour. Using tongs, transfer the oxtails to a large bowl and place the roasting pan over two stove burners. Reduce the oven temperature to 350°F.

Add the curry powder, shrimp paste, cardamom, garlic, star anise, cloves, lime leaves, bell peppers, lemongrass, cinnamon stick, curry sprig, onion, and ginger to the roasting pan, and cook over medium heat, stirring occasionally, until the vegetables are softened, about 25 minutes. Return the oxtails to the pan and add the tomatoes, coconut milk, and just enough water to cover the oxtails—4 to 5 cups, depending on the size and shape of your pan. Bring the liquid to a simmer, then remove the pan from the heat, cover with foil, return to the oven, and cook until the oxtails are tender and falling off the bone, about 3 hours.

Remove the pan from the oven, uncover, and season to taste with lime juice and fish sauce. Serve hot with chopped cilantro and mint on top, lime wedges on the side, and plenty of roti bread for soaking up the juices.

oxtail curry with roti, cont'd

Roti MAKES 12

Olive oil, for greasing and shaping the dough

1 cup all-purpose flour, plus more for dusting

1 cup pastry flour

1 teaspoon kosher salt

1 teaspoon granulated sugar

½ teaspoon baking powder

½ cup crème fraîche

½ cup plain whole-milk yogurt

About ¾ cup ghee or clarified butter

Line a baking sheet with parchment paper and lightly oil the paper. Combine the flours, salt, sugar, and baking powder in a bowl. In a separate large bowl, combine the crème fraîche and yogurt. Add the dry ingredients, stir, and knead until combined. Transfer the dough to a lightly floured work surface and knead until smooth, about 8 minutes. Divide the dough into 12 equal-sized pieces, form each into a tight ball, and place the balls on the prepared baking sheet. Brush the dough balls with oil, cover with plastic wrap, and refrigerate overnight.

Remove the dough balls from the fridge 30 minutes before cooking. Oil two sheets of parchment paper and a second baking sheet. Set 1 dough ball on an oiled parchment sheet, then cover second with the oiled parchment sheet; keep the remaining dough balls covered with plasteic wrap. Using a rolling pin, roll out the dough ⅓ inch thick (the shape doesn't matter), set it on the oiled baking sheet, and cover with plastic wrap. Repeat with the remaining dough balls, stacking the rolled pieces of dough on top of each other on the baking sheet as they are finished.

Heat 1 tablespoon ghee in a 12-inch cast-iron skillet over high. Add 1 roti to the pan and cook, flipping once, until lightly charred on both sides, about 2 minutes total. Transfer to a serving platter. Cook the remaining roti in the same way, adding more ghee to the pan as needed.

The Chef's Chef

NEW YORK, NEW YORK

Celebrity chefs go on TV. Great chefs run kitchens. So there's a chance you may not have heard of Tien Ho, an OG kitchen warrior revered by virtually everyone he's ever worked with. He spent years in the David Chang fold, the talent incubator of the aughts, and several of the most-famous Momofuku, Inc. dishes (like the can't-stop-eating-them rice cakes with spicy pork ragu that will never leave Ssäm Bar's menu) bear his fingerprints. He's also a longtime friend of MUNCHIES and helped us design our test kitchen.

He's such a kitchen legend that no one even begrudged him when he moved away from the line and toward the C-suite. (As of this writing, he's global vice president of culinary and hospitality at Whole Foods.) But his ridiculously good Vietnamese spinoff of pâté en croûte proves that, while you may be able to take the chef out of the kitchen, you can't take the kitchen out of the chef.

This version, which we refer to as meat pie, is like a humblebrag in food form. It's peasant food that actually requires real skill to make. But don't worry—Tien's got you. His has all the magic of the French original, but without the stress. The welcome addition of lemongrass, licorice-y purple-stemmed basil, and fish sauce is the Vietnamese-born chef's riff on the classic. It's the colonial influence on Vietnamese food with the script flipped.

FILLING

4¼ pounds ground pork, well chilled

1 pound 5 ounces pork fatback, ground (ask your butcher to do this) and well chilled

2 cups finely chopped fresh basil leaves

½ cup minced garlic

½ cup minced lemongrass

½ cup minced shallots

⅓ cup kosher salt

¼ cup nonfat dry milk powder

2 tablespoons fish sauce

2 tablespoons Sriracha

1 tablespoon granulated sugar

¼ teaspoon pink curing salt #1

PASTRY

3½ cups plus 2 tablespoons all-purpose flour

1 tablespoon kosher salt

1 cup (2 sticks) plus 1½ tablespoons cold unsalted butter, cut into ½-inch cubes, plus more for greasing

2 large eggs, lightly beaten

1 cup ice-cold water, plus more if needed

1 large egg mixed with 2 tablespoons heavy cream

Lemongrass and Thai Basil Pork Pie   SERVES 8

To make the filling, combine all the ingredients in the bowl of a stand mixer fitted with a paddle attachment and mix on medium speed until smooth, about 5 to 7 minutes. Cover the bowl with plastic wrap and refrigerate for at least 24 hours.

While the meat rests, make the pastry. In a food processor, combine the flour, salt, and butter and pulse until the mixture has a sandy texture, about 10 pulses. Add the eggs and ice water and pulse until a dough forms, adding more water by the tablespoonful if the mixture is too dry. Transfer the dough to a work surface. Form it into a large ball, then divide in two and form each half into a 1-inch-thick disk. Wrap each disk in plastic wrap and refrigerate for 1 hour.

Heat the oven to 350°F. Grease a 10-inch round springform pan with butter. On a lightly floured work surface, use a rolling pin to roll out each dough disk to ¼-inch-thick circle. Transfer one to the prepared pan, settling it in the bottom and up the sides, letting the excess hang over the edge. Fill with the filling and cover with the other sheet of dough. Trim the excess dough from the edge of the pie, then crimp the edges to seal. Cut a hole in the center of the pie with a 1-inch round cutter, then knead together the trimmed scraps of dough, roll out, and cut out leaves, vines, and other shapes to decorate the top crust. Brush the top crust with some of the egg-cream wash, attach the decorations, then brush the decorations with egg wash.

Bake the pie until an instant-read thermometer inserted into the center reads 140°F, 1½ to 2 hours. Let cool on a wire rack, then remove the outer ring. Serve the pie at room temperature.

Roberta's

BROOKLYN, NEW YORK

Convincing Manhattanites to take the L train to Morgan Avenue for pizza is a feat on a par with persuading them to drop $6K a month for an apartment in New Jersey. But that's exactly what Carlo Mirarchi did when he and his partners opened Roberta's, the free-wheeling wood-oven pizza place that opened in an industrial corner of Bushwick before people opened wood-oven pizza places in industrial corners of Bushwick. What started as a clubhouse of Brooklyn chill serving gonzo Neapolitan pies with names like Cheesus Christ and Axl Rosenberg evolved into a Brooklandian compound with a wholesale bakery, on-premises food-focused radio station, and twelve-seat high-concept hipster omakase bar called Blanca.

On his episode of *Chef's Night Out*, Carlo toured a greatest-hits list of NYC's restaurants, killing several bottles at low-key natural wine heaven Ten Bells on the Lower East Side, crushing duck carnitas at Cosme, and eating all the things at Mission Chinese Food, all before reuniting at Blanca with current and former Roberta's staff for wine, steaks, and this ridiculous porchetta.

This is basically the king of dinner party food: it's a pork roast made entirely out of bacon. Sure, it takes time—a day to brine, a good six or so hours to roast—but most of that time is spent waiting, and the payoff is immense: it's all shattery-crisp golden skin and juicy flesh, the kind of dish you haul out to a chorus of "Oohs," "Aahs," and "Damns." The secrets to Mirarchi's version are legion, but one is surely the combo of the traditional core of herbs and those same herbs mixed with salt then rubbed on the skin. The addition of fennel pollen is another, since it is to the typical fennel seed in porchetta what Roberta's pizza is to Sbarro's.

PORK AND BRINE

1½ cups granulated sugar

1 cup kosher salt

1 (10-pound) piece skin-on pork belly

12 cups ice-cold water

PORCHETTA RUB

½ cup roughly chopped fresh rosemary leaves

¼ cup roughly chopped fresh sage leaves

1½ tablespoons fennel pollen

2 teaspoons kosher salt

1 teaspoon freshly ground black pepper

6 cloves garlic, roughly chopped

4 Meyer lemons (or small, thin-skinned regular lemons), halved, seeds removed, and roughly chopped

PORCHETTA SALT

¾ cup plus 1 tablespoon kosher salt

¼ cup dried rosemary

¼ cup fennel pollen

2½ tablespoons fennel seeds

1½ teaspoons Piment d'Espelette powder

1 teaspoon ground dried sage

Finely grated zest of 3 lemons

Porchetta SERVES 12 TO 20

To brine the pork belly, combine the sugar, salt, and 4 cups water in a medium saucepan and bring to a boil, stirring to dissolve the sugar and salt. Remove from the heat and pour into a container large enough to hold the pork belly. Add the ice-cold water and stir until cool. Submerge the pork belly in the brine, cover with plastic wrap, and refrigerate for at least 24 hours.

Meanwhile, to make the porchetta rub, combine all the ingredients in a food processor and pulse until finely chopped. Transfer to an airtight container and refrigerate until ready to use. Wipe out the food processor. To make the porchetta salt add all the ingredients to the food processor and pulse until evenly ground. Transfer the salt to an airtight container and store at room temperature until ready to use.

Heat the oven to 250°F. Remove the pork belly from the brine, dry thoroughly with paper towels, then evenly rub the meat side with the porchetta rub mixture. Roll up the pork belly lengthwise, jelly roll–style, into a tight cylinder. Using six to eight 12-inch lengths of kitchen twine, tie a length of string around the rolled belly every 2 inches, knotting to secure. Rub the porchetta salt all over the tied pork belly, then place on a wire rack set in a roasting pan. Bake the porchetta until an instant-read thermometer inserted in the middle reads 185°F, about 4 hours.

Transfer the rack with the porchetta to a cutting board and let rest for 1 hour. Drain off the pan juices and reserve. Increase the oven temperature to 450°F, then return the rack with the porchetta to the roasting pan, place back in the oven, and roast until the skin is golden, puffed, and crisp, about 30 minutes. Transfer the porchetta to a cutting board and let rest for 15 minutes. Remove the twine, slice, and serve with the pan juices.

Frank Castronovo and Frank Falcinelli—The Franks—have basically defined the fancy-home-cooking-in-the-cozy-space-you-wish-you-could-afford-to-live-in restaurant movement. Not that they'd accept that title. They're just chill, soft-spoken dudes who happen to make damn good food.

And if you were a chill, soft-spoken dude who made damn good food and also happened to be connected to the New York food mob, you'd also eat perfect pizza at Roberta's, then smoke a joint outside after. And you'd chase that with more perfect pizza (and high-end fried bologna) at Motorino. You'd probably also kidnap Motorino's chef and bring him back to your restaurant (smoking more weed en route) and feed him these meatballs.

SAUCE

½ cup olive oil

6 garlic cloves

Large pinch of crushed red pepper flakes

2 (28-ounce) cans whole peeled tomatoes, crushed by hand

4 teaspoons fine sea salt

MEATBALLS

4 slices bread
(2 packed cups' worth)

2 pounds ground beef

3 cloves garlic, minced

¼ cup finely chopped fresh flat-leaf parsley

¼ cup grated Pecorino Romano

¼ cup raisins

¼ cup pine nuts

1½ teaspoons fine sea salt

15 cranks white pepper

4 large eggs

½ cup plain dried breadcrumbs, plus more if needed

Grated Pecorino Romano, for serving

Meatballs and Red Sauce SERVES 6

To make the sauce, heat the olive oil in a Dutch oven over medium-low. Add the garlic and cook, stirring occasionally, until the garlic is deeply colored and fragrant, about 10 minutes. Add the red pepper flakes and cook for about 30 seconds to infuse the oil. Add the tomatoes and salt and stir well. Turn down the heat to medium and allow the sauce to simmer, stirring every so often, for about 4 hours. Taste for salt and keep warm.

To make the meatballs, heat the oven to 325°F. Put the bread slices in a bowl, cover it with water, and let it soak for a minute or so. Pour off the water and wring out the bread, then tear it into tiny pieces. in a medium mixing bowl, combine the bread with all of the remaining meatball ingredients. The mixture

should be moist, not sloppy wet, add more crumbs if needed.

Shape the meat mixture into handball-sized meatballs and space them evenly on a baking sheet. Bake for 25 to 30 minutes. When the meatballs are cooked through, they will be firm but still juicy and gently yielding. (At this point, you can cool the meatballs and hold them in the refrigerator for as long as a couple of days or you can freeze them.)

Add the meatballs to the pan of warm tomato sauce, increase the heat ever so slightly, and simmer for 30 minutes or so so they can soak up some of the sauce. Serve the meatballs with a healthy helping of the sauce and hit each portion (not the pan) with a fluffy mountain of grated cheese.

Raconteur

NEW YORK, NEW YORK

Anthony Bourdain was leading us on a brass-knuckled tour of New York with the crew of his TV show *No Reservations* in tow. These were the heady days before the show turned the culinary swashbuckler from food-world luminary into bonafide celebrity with a show on CNN and a line of action figures (probably). Since then, Bourdain has become a sort of gastro-Hemingway, a heavy-drinking word-smith who did battle for years in the kitchen (and with heroin addiction, but who's counting). It left him with the swagger and leathery face of a man who's lived a good, hard life. Nowadays, Tony—can we call you Tony? No? Oh—Bourdain is tough to catch out of character, so we joined him for too many drinks to witness his true colors. Which turned out to be blood red.

Bourdain's uber-carnivore vibe is no shtick: The guy really fucking loves the pleasures of the (animal) flesh. And when he drinks, he loves the flesh even more than usual—evidenced by the platter of cured meat at Salumeria Rosi, the Upper West Side restaurant run by his friend Cesare Casella, also known as the Wonderful Wizard of Meat. Bourdain and company even pulled out their phones to snap pics of the mortadella and coppa, like a bunch of tweens.

And what else did we learn about Bourdain while he was drunk? The heart wants what it wants, and it turns out Bourdain's heart really wants the Distinguished Wakamba Lounge, a time-warp Dominican dive bar—as bumping as its more common Irish counterparts are melancholy—in the grimy region near Penn Station. The place serves up little more than Presidente, whiskey, and nostalgia—a vision of Manhattan before the invasion of Bank of America, Starbucks, and Chipotle. No wonder he calls it his "special place."

Bourdain was slurring in the van as they headed toward his old base of operations, Brasserie Les Halles, the restaurant he ran before he blew up. In the kitchen, where the mostly Latino line cooks turned out pitch-perfect steak tartare and frisee aux lardons, he started cooking cote de boeuf, better known in English as huge rib steaks, and the cooks razzed him. Admittedly he hadn't cooked in a restaurant kitchen for many years, but his chef de cuisine, the late Carlos Llaguno Garcia, finished the monstrous steaks, carving perfectly bloody slices from the charred slabs of beef. Well done, Tony.

Take it from Tony: "Keep in mind that this is a big, fat piece of meat that's been in the refrigerator a long time and is hence chilled to the bone. Particularly if you plan on cooking this rare or medium rare (and you'd better be), you want to get that chill out. So pull those big, beautiful beasts out of the fridge a good half hour before cooking time and let them come up to room temperature. Make sure you have the following equipment readily available: An outdoor grill or grill pan, a brush, tongs, a roasting pan, a cutting board, a very sharp, badass-looking knife, a serving platter, and a novelty apron or vintage Ted Nugent T-shirt." He suggests serving this accompanied by béarnaise sauce, French fries, and a staggeringly expensive bottle of Burgundy in cheap glasses.

2 (34-ounce) bone-in rib steaks, at room temperature

Kosher salt and freshly ground black pepper

Côte de Bœuf   SERVES 2

Heat a grill or grill pan to high heat, and heat the oven to 400°F. (This cut is just too damn thick to cook all the way on the grill.)

Season the steaks on both sides with salt and pepper. Sear both steaks on the grill or in a grill pan. Turn them 180 degrees on each side to get that cool checkerboard pattern we all like, and continue grilling on both sides until they have a nice brown crust, about 5 to 7 minutes.

Now toss those bad boys into the roasting pan and finish them in the oven. It should be about 8 to 10 minutes for medium rare, depending on the thickness of the steaks.

When the steaks are cooked to your desired doneness, transfer them to a cutting board and allow them to rest for a good 10 minutes. They don't have to be served sizzling hot; in fact, they shouldn't be—it's much more important that all those lovely juices distribute internally. Do not poke. Do not slice. Do not molest until the steaks are well rested.

Bring the steaks on the cutting board to the table. Wielding your razor-sharp slicing knife and with terrifying aplomb, slice and serve up great bleeding, fat-rippled hunks.

CHAPTER 7

Dessert

The Meatball Shop

NEW YORK, NEW YORK

Read enough about restaurants (particularly during the past decade, when food mags entered their Spanish and Danish periods) and it seems like for chefs to get love, they've got to push the envelope. Not Michael Chernow and Daniel Holzman. These two native New Yorkers don't mess around with dehydrated lichen or foraged borage. Instead, they found success rethinking the meatball. That is, they took everyone's favorite thing about Italian-American food and built an empire around it. Now you can barely make it ten blocks in their hometown without running into the Meatball Shop (seven locations and counting), where you can get all manner of delectable orbs in many forms—sliders or heroes, on pasta or polenta, and the best-selling kitchen-sink salad, which is basically every vegetable the cooks can find mixed with meatballs and some sauce on top. If this qualifies as salad, consider us health nuts.

While it's never too late at night for meatballs, when these chefs were tasked with feeding a horde of friends, they veered from their signature dish. Instead, they made ice cream sandwiches, which are kind of like the meatballs of dessert. Not everything has to expand your mind.

MINT ICE CREAM

2½ cups whole milk

1⅓ cups granulated sugar

1 small bunch fresh mint, plus 1 cup finely chopped fresh mint leaves

3 cups heavy cream

1½ teaspoons vanilla extract

7 large egg yolks

CHOCOLATE CHIP COOKIES

½ cup (1 stick) unsalted butter

⅓ cup firmly packed dark brown sugar

1 cup granulated sugar

1 large egg

1 large egg white

2 teaspoons vanilla extract

2 cups all-purpose flour

1 teaspoon baking soda

1 teaspoon kosher salt

2½ cups semisweet chocolate chips, finely chopped

Chocolate Chip and Mint Ice Cream Sandwiches
MAKES 2½ DOZEN COOKIE SANDWICHES

To make the ice cream, bring the milk, half of the sugar, and the bunch of mint to a boil in a medium pot over medium heat, stirring frequently to dissolve the sugar. Once the mixture boils, remove from the heat and let steep for 30 minutes. Combine the cream, vanilla, and the chopped mint in a large bowl and set aside.

Remove the bunch of mint from the pot and bring the mixture back up to a boil, then reduce the heat to low. In a large bowl, whisk the egg yolks with the remaining sugar. Temper the yolks by slowly drizzling in 1 cup of the hot milk mixture while whisking vigorously. Slowly pour the tempered eggs into the pot of hot milk and cook over low heat, stirring constantly, until the mixture begins to thicken, coats the back of a metal spoon, and reaches 170°F on an instant-read thermometer. (The mixture can easily overcook and curdle, so be sure not to bring it to a boil.) Strain the mixture through a fine sieve into the bowl with the cream, vanilla, and chopped mint and stir to combine. Cover with plastic wrap and refrigerate the custard until well chilled, then freeze in an ice-cream maker according to the manufacturer's instructions, working in batches if necessary. Transfer the ice cream to an airtight container and freeze for at least 4 hours.

To make the cookies, using an electric mixer, cream the butter, brown sugar, and granulated sugar in a stand mixer on high speed until light and fluffy, about 3 minutes. Add the egg, egg white, and vanilla and mix on low speed until just incorporated. In a medium bowl, whisk together the flour, baking soda, and salt. Add the flour mixture to the butter mixture and mix on low speed, until just combined. (Do not overmix.) Fold in the chocolate chips with a wooden spoon or rubber spatula. Cover the dough with plastic wrap and refrigerate for 30 minutes.

Heat the oven to 350°F with the racks in the top and bottom thirds of the oven and line two baking sheets with parchment paper. Using a 1-ounce ice-cream scooper, scoop the dough into 1-inch balls and place on the prepared sheets, spacing the balls 2 inches apart. Bake, rotating the pans halfway through baking, until the edges of the cookies are golden brown but the centers are soft, about 12 minutes. Let the cookies cool on the baking sheets for 2 minutes, then transfer them with a spatula to wire racks and let cool completely.

Sandwich scoops of mint ice cream between cookies. Wrap each ice cream sandwich in plastic wrap and freeze for at least 4 hours or up to 24 hours before serving.

Rajat Parr is—if you'll pardon the wine-dork interlude—your favorite sommelier's favorite sommelier. From his throne as the wine director of the Michael Mina restaurant empire, the Calcutta-born legend of the rotten-grape game led the charge for vibrant, food-friendly American wine. He's a big part of why you're not drinking those high-alcohol California monsters that ruled back in the day. He's since shed his tastevin to become a winemaker, blessing the world with Sandhi Wines and producing cult-favorite small-batch Pinot Noir from the hills of Santa Rita. The French might get mad when you call not-from-Burgundy wines Burgundian, but there's really no other word for what he's making—high-acid, intensely minerally juice that works with pretty much almost all food. But trust us: wait until the wine bottles are empty before you eat this ultra-rich spiced rice pudding. If you're still thirsty, Parr suggests rocking glasses of calvados while you dig in. We prefer ours with a pair of fat pants.

Cardamom Rice Pudding   SERVES 6 TO 8

3 cups heavy cream

2 cups whole milk

½ cup granulated sugar

4 cardamom pods, cracked open

2 cinnamon sticks

Zest strips from ½ orange

1 vanilla bean, split

¾ cup plus 2 tablespoons basmati or jasmine rice

4 large egg yolks

Seasonal fresh fruit of your choice

Combine 2 cups of the cream, the milk, sugar, cardamom, cinnamon sticks, and orange zest strips in a large saucepan. Use a knife to scrape the seeds from the vanilla bean into the saucepan and add the pod halves, too. Bring to a simmer over medium heat, stirring to dissolve the sugar. Remove from the heat and let steep for 20 minutes.

Pour the mixture through a fine sieve into a bowl, discard the aromatics, and return the mixture to the pan. Bring to a gentle simmer, then add the rice, reduce the heat to low, and cook, stirring occasionally, until the rice is very tender and the mixture has thickened, about 30 minutes. Remove the pan from the heat and whisk in the yolks. Transfer the rice pudding to a large bowl and cover the surface directly with plastic wrap. Refrigerate until chilled, at least 4 hours.

In a bowl, beat the remaining 1 cup of cream until stiff peaks form. Remove the pudding from the refrigerator, add the whipped cream, and fold until lightened. Serve at once with fresh seasonal fruit.

Ovenly

BROOKLYN, NEW YORK

Agatha Kulaga and Erin Patinkin, the self-taught bakers behind Brooklyn sweet/salty treat operation Ovenly, built their business from the ground up, leaving the social justice and social work worlds for the sweet one. Being progressive is still their jam, though: they partner with nonprofit organizations to provide jobs and training for refugees and the previously incarcerated. Watching them eat nachos and old-school donuts, and otherwise do their thing with a crew of women-in-food, is the epitome of #squadgoals.

Dark cocoa powder (which you may have to mail-order) and pudding-spiked buttercream are the keys to this super-dark chocolate cake. Milk is a nice accompaniment, but Kulaga and Patinkin personally paired it with a shit-ton of Old Crow, drunk straight out of the bottle. Blackout Cake, indeed.

CAKE

1½ cups Brooklyn Brewery Black Chocolate Stout or other chocolate stout

1½ cups (3 sticks) unsalted butter, cut into ½-inch pieces, plus more for greasing

1½ cups Dutch-processed cocoa powder

3 cups all-purpose flour, plus more for dusting

2¾ cups granulated sugar

2¼ teaspoons baking soda

1½ teaspoons kosher salt

1 cup sour cream

3 large eggs, at room temperature

BUTTERCREAM

¾ cup Salted Dark Chocolate Pudding (page 210)

1 cup (2 sticks) unsalted butter, cubed and at room temperature

7 cups confectioners' sugar, plus more as needed

½ cup Dutch-process cocoa powder

¼ teaspoon kosher salt

Heavy cream, if needed

Blackout Stout Cake   SERVES 8 TO 10

To make the cake, heat the oven to 350°F. Grease two 9-inch round cake pans with butter. Line the bottoms with parchment rounds, grease the rounds, and dust the pans with flour, knocking out the excess.

In a large, heavy saucepan over medium heat, bring the stout and butter to a simmer. Remove the pan from the heat, add the cocoa powder, and whisk until the mixture is smooth. Let cool for 5 minutes.

While the stout-butter mixture cools, in a large bowl whisk together the flour, sugar, baking soda, and salt.

In a separate large bowl, whisk together the sour cream and eggs.

Add the stout-butter mixture to the egg mixture and whisk to combine. Add the flour mixture and combine with a rubber spatula until all the ingredients are incorporated and the batter is smooth. Be sure to scrape the bottom of the bowl to incorporate any dry, floury bits.

Divide the batter equally between the prepared cake pans. Bake for 35 to 40 minutes, until a toothpick inserted in the center of each layer comes out clean. Transfer to a wire rack to cool.

To make the buttercream, in the bowl of a stand mixer fitted with a paddle attachment, combine the salted dark chocolate pudding, the butter, 3 cups of the confectioners' sugar, the cocoa powder, and the salt and mix on low until just incorporated. Increase the speed to medium-high and beat until the ingredients are well combined and the mixture is creamy, about 1 minute. Scrape down the sides of the bowl with a rubber spatula.

Add more confectioners' sugar, up to 1 cup at a time, mixing on low speed for 1 minute after each addition, until the mixture is thick but spreadable. You may not need to add all the remaining sugar, but you will need most of it. Once you have the correct consistency, scrape down the sides of the bowl. Raise the speed to medium-high, and beat for 3 to 4 minutes, *blackout stout cake, cont'd*

or until the buttercream is very light and fluffy, but thick enough to spread. If it is too thick, beat in a little more cream. If it is too thin, add a little more confectioners' sugar.

To assemble the cake, place one cake layer on a cake stand or platter. Top with about one third of the buttercream and spread the buttercream into an even layer. Place the second cake on top. Frost the top and sides of the stacked cake with the remaining frosting.

Salted Dark Chocolate Pudding MAKES 2 CUPS

2 cups whole milk

2 ½ tablespoons cornstarch

½ cup sugar

2 ounces (about ⅓ cup) dark chocolate, chopped

3 tablespoons Dutch-processed cocoa powder

1 teaspoon vanilla extract

¾ teaspoon fine sea salt

In a small bowl, whisk together ¼ cup of the whole milk and the cornstarch until smooth.

In a medium saucepan, combine the remaining 1¾ cups milk, sugar, dark chocolate, cocoa powder, vanilla, and sea salt. Heat over medium-low, whisking, until the chocolate is melted.

Whisk the cornstarch mixture into the chocolate mixture until fully incorporated.

Turn the heat to low, and continue to stir briskly with a wooden spoon or a heatproof spatula. The mixture will come to a simmer and will slowly begin to thicken.

Continue to cook for 1 to 2 minutes, until the pudding coats the back of the spoon and slowly drips off. The pudding will be thick and just starting to bubble. Remove the pudding from the heat and cover it by placing plastic wrap directly on the pudding so that a skin doesn't form. Refrigerate for at least 1 hour or until set. Stored airtight in the refrigerator, the pudding will keep for 5 days.

Lazy Bear

SAN FRANCISCO, CALIFORNIA

Maya Erickson is insanely young and insanely talented, a combo that in the culinary world might as well be shorthand for "can party like an animal." She started her career staging with punk pastry goddess Elizabeth Falkner at sixteen (as one does), landed a job with her straight out of high school, and has been crushing it ever since. She's bounced around from great kitchen to great kitchen, leaving behind only good feelings and memories of stunning desserts. Her creations are stark multi part landscapes with unexpected ingredients (like *shio koji* or bay leaves) that hit every part of your pleasure centers; her *mignardises* (the mini-desserts a pastry chef must have in her arsenal), meanwhile, take the familiar (pb&j or s'mores) and fuck with it until it's exactly what you remember but way better.

And about that partying: you might think that once our cameras shut off, that's it; everyone goes home and goes to bed. But not with Erickson. Around 4 a.m., she was going so hard her boss kicked us out of Lazy Bear, the San Francisco restaurant where she was pastry chef at the time—earlier in the evening, he'd announced he was "the dad around here" and this was indeed a classic dad move. After our entrance to a local strip club was rebuffed, we ended up in a rented limo driving back and forth over the Golden Gate Bridge until a new foggy day had dawned.

MAYA ERICKSON

As chef Erickson put it, "It's a pretty standard recipe." Yeah, maybe it's standard for you, chef. This salty-sweet-bitter combo of everyone's favorite Italian digestif and PETA's favorite charcuterie blew our minds and put in sharp focus precisely why you're awesome.

Fernet Gingerbread with Foie Gras Torchon SERVES 6 TO 8

1 cup molasses

½ cup Guinness or other stout

⅓ cup Fernet-Branca

1½ teaspoons baking soda

1 (4-inch) piece ginger, peeled and grated

1¼ cups granulated sugar

1 cup peanut oil

2 large eggs

2½ cups all-purpose flour

1½ teaspoons kosher salt

¾ teaspoon ground cinnamon

½ teaspoon ground ginger

¼ teaspoon ground cloves

5 ounces foie gras torchon, sliced ¼-inch thick

Fresh flat-leaf parsley, for garnish

Heat the oven to 350°F. Grease a 13 by 18-inch baking sheet and line it with parchment paper. In a medium saucepan, bring the molasses, beer, and Fernet to a boil. Remove from heat, add the baking soda, and whisk well (careful—this will bubble up quite a bit), then add the grated ginger.

In a large bowl, whisk together the sugar, oil, and eggs. Into a separate bowl, sift together the flour, salt, and spices. Alternate whisking the dry ingredients and the molasses mixture into the egg and oil mixture until combined.

Pour the batter into the prepared baking sheet and spread into an even layer. Bake until a toothpick inserted in the center comes out clean, 15 to 20 minutes. Let the gingerbread cool completely in the pan on a wire rack.

Cut the gingerbread into 1 by 3-inch pieces and top each with a piece of the foie gras. Serve garnished with parsley.

Le Bal Café

PARIS, FRANCE

It takes bollocks for two Brits to open a café in Paris, and Anna Trattles and Alice Quillet each have a massive set.

Figuratively, of course. The duo is part of the cadre of culinary revolutionaries who are transforming the city's restaurant scene from an untouchable constellation of Michelin stars into a place where you can dine well without feeling like you've paid for a trip into space. Anna and Alice have managed to win over Parisians without resorting to steak frites and coquille St. Jacques. Even more incredible, they don't run from the cuisine that brought us mushy peas and the dish of pig innards wrapped in caul fat called faggots. At their pint-size spot down a cobblestone alley in the eighteenth arrondissement, they embrace their heritage with pork pies, coronation chicken, and sticky toffee pudding while channeling the ingredient-driven simplicity of French café fare.

The night we met them, they pregamed, like good Englishwomen, with a pitcher of Pimm's Cup, followed by a low-key rager that starts, as all good nights should, with lamb's head. Trattles and Quillet are drawn to other expats in Paris. That lamb's head, for instance, was cooked by Aussie and Le Bal brunch regular chef James Henry, who used to head up the kitchen at cool-kids restaurant Bones (RIP). Then, at Mary Celeste, they hung out with Haan Palcu-Chang (half Chinese, just like Trattles)

who served them a beet dish so French looking you wouldn't realize it's a riff on Cantonese turnip cakes until you'd bitten into the blood-red cubes, crispy on the outside and springy within. But Trattles and Quillet aren't only about expat living and neo-French fare. To end the night, they kept things *très français* at Chez Ammad, a quintessential Montmartre bar that Anna described as, how do you say . . . "shitty." But in the best way. There, they imbibed in a highly traditional French fashion—with far too many Jameson shots.

As far as we know, the French government won't give foreign cooks a work visa unless they can make a proper *tarte au citron*. Since the ladies of Le Bal Café have been in the City of Light for a minute, we assumed they'd have a recipe worth making. That was true times ten, which we learned when they tricked out the typical tart made with lemon curd (sugar for sweetness, juice for tartness, zest for flavor, and eggs for the custardy texture), topping it with a sort of coconut-almond crumble that bakes into the curd. They finished it with a drizzle of lemon juice-and-sugar icing that we have taken to drizzling over every tart we make, from apple to quince.

PASTRY

2 large egg yolks

1 large egg

1 teaspoon vanilla extract

3 cups all-purpose flour, plus more for dusting

½ cup granulated sugar

20 tablespoons (2½ sticks) cold unsalted butter, cubed

1 teaspoon kosher salt

1 large egg white, lightly beaten

LEMON CURD

1½ cups granulated sugar

6 tablespoons unsalted butter

Finely grated zest and juice of 6 lemons

6 large eggs

3 large egg yolks

FILLING

18 tablespoons (2¼ sticks) unsalted butter, at room temperature

1¼ cups superfine sugar

6 large eggs, at room temperature

1 cup ground almonds or almond meal

2 cups shredded unsweetened coconut

1½ tablespoons all-purpose flour

Finely grated zest of 3 lemons

TO FINISH

2 cups confectioners' sugar

3 tablespoons freshly squeezed lemon juice

1 tablespoon shredded unsweetened coconut, toasted

Finely grated zest of 1 lemon

Toasted Coconut–Lemon Curd Tart

MAKES 2 (9-INCH) TARTS

To make the pastry, in a small bowl, whisk together the egg yolks, whole egg, and vanilla. In a food processor, pulse the flour, sugar, butter, and salt into a coarse meal. Transfer to a large bowl and add the egg mixture. With a fork, gradually incorporate the egg mixture into the flour mixture, then use your hands to bring it all together into a cohesive dough; if the dough is too dry to hold together, add a tablespoon or two of water. Divide the dough into two balls, wrap each ball in plastic wrap, and refrigerate for at least 1 hour.

To make the lemon curd, put the sugar, butter, and lemon zest and juice in a medium bowl. Set the bowl over a pan of simmering water, making sure the water is not touching the bowl. Stir the mixture until all the butter has melted, then remove the bowl from the pan.

In a second medium bowl, lightly whisk the whole eggs and egg yolks. Slowly stir about one-third of the warm butter mixture into the eggs, then stir that mixture into the remaining butter mixture. Return the bowl to the pan of simmering water and cook, stirring constantly, until the lemon curd is thick and creamy, about 17 minutes. Pour the curd through a fine sieve set over a clean bowl. Let cool, cover, and refrigerate until ready to use.

To make the filling, in a stand mixer fitted with a paddle attachment, beat the butter and sugar until light and fluffy. Add the eggs and mix well. Gently fold in the ground almonds, coconut, flour, and zest. Transfer to a pastry bag.

Heat the oven to 375°F. On a lightly floured surface, roll out one ball of dough into a 12-inch circle. Gently transfer to a 9-inch tart pan with a removable bottom and press into the bottom and the sides. Cover the surface with a sheet of parchment paper and fill with beans or rice. Repeat with the other ball of dough. Bake the tart shells for 15 minutes, then remove the beans and bake for an additional 12 minutes until lightly golden. Brush the shells with the egg white and bake 1 minute longer. Let the shells cool slightly.

Divide the lemon curd between the shells. Pipe the filling over the curd in concentric rings. Bake the tarts for 30 to 35 minutes, or until the filling is golden and slightly wobbly. Let cool completely.

Put the confectioners' sugar in a medium bowl. Slowly mix in the lemon juice to make a thick but pourable icing. Drizzle the icing over the tarts and sprinkle with the coconut and lemon zest.

CHAPTER 8

The Morning After

Tacos Punta Cabras

LOS ANGELES, CALIFORNIA

To so many people, Baja still conjures faux Mexican salads with romaine and tortilla strips rather than the spectacularly beautiful Mexican peninsula jutting into the Pacific or the thrilling seafood-heavy food you find there. Josh Gil and his long-time culinary collaborator Daniel Snukal get it. The two took their fancy restaurant pedigrees, said "Fuck it," and opened up Tacos Punta Cabras, a shack in Santa Monica serving a handful of killer tostadas, *cocteles*, and tacos—of the kind and the quality you'd find a few hours south. Seriously, they're legit, for those of you who think praising tacos on L.A.'s Westside is like giving props to the pad thai in Moscow. Gil and Snukal do things right: Flour tortillas are house-made (and well made, which is not necessarily the same thing); the seafood—some of which is battered and deep-fried—is dumb fresh, in the Ensenada mold; and the condiments, like cabbage slaw and salsas, provide the right heat and acidity to make Eastsiders schlep to the coast at last.

When they cooked for their friends, they busted out tacos that would be at home on either side of the Beautiful Border Wall. They merged the flour-tortilla-and-egg perfection of an Austin breakfast taco with the rich, briny funk of sea urchin, which you'd find at both L.A.'s top sushi spots and Baja's best street vendors. As the chefs advise, use as much as you can afford, which, trust us, will prevent you from using too much. Sea urchin is expensive, after all, thanks to whatever dark-humored sea god decided to make urchin gonads into the most luscious, sweet-and-briny custard imaginable and then encase them in spiky armor. Getting at the good stuff is hard work. Luckily, as with every task in the twenty-first century, someone can do it for you.

UNI

UNI

D'Antaño
TEQUILA 100% AGAVE

Nowadays, many fine fishmongers sell whole, live sea urchins, which allows for the dramatic presentation you see in the photo at left. Of course, buying them whole means you must jimmy them open and de-gonad the ocean freak. So for novices, we recommend the small wooden trays piled with the yellow-orange lobes, like a heap of disembodied cat tongues, of what's euphemistically called "roe." Keep in mind that sea urchins from the waters off California tend to be sweeter and pricier, while those from Maine are brinier and less expensive. Ultimately, it's a preference thing—you can't really go wrong either way.

Scrambled Eggs with Uni SERVES 2

1 tablespoon clarified butter

½ yellow onion, diced

6 large eggs, lightly beaten

2 tablespoons crème fraîche

Kosher salt and freshly ground black pepper

Flour tortillas, warmed

Uni (as much as you can afford)

1 avocado, pitted, peeled, and thinly sliced (optional)

Sliced scallions, for serving

Hot sauce, for serving

In a 10-inch skillet, heat the butter over medium-low. Add the onion and cook, stirring occassionally, until softened, 5 to 7 minutes. Add the eggs and cook, stirring constantly with a wooden spoon and breaking up the curds, until the eggs are almost set, 3 to 4 minutes. Add the crème fraîche, season with salt and pepper, and cook 1 to 2 minutes longer. Divide among the tortillas and top with the uni and avocado slices, sprinkle with scallions, and serve with hot sauce.

While the food media was collectively shitting its shorts over the hot hot hot trend from England where chefs served tasty, creative food without the pomp of white tablecloths and fine stemware, some of us were drinking Sapporo, eating oysters gratinéed with mayo and grilled soy-marinated fish collars, and wondering if *gastropub* wasn't just another word for "izakaya." In Vancouver and Toronto, the hubs of Canada's Japanese population, Guu Izakaya is the Spotted Pig of Japanese pub food—an early ambassador of an easygoing, boldly flavored kind of food and one that still rocks after more than a decade. Just as you find yourself at izakayas indulging in classics you didn't know were classics—like *takowasa* (wasabi-marinated raw octopus) or pumpkin croquettes—Guu director of operations Masaru Ogasawara welcomed us into his kitchen for a hangover cure we didn't know was a hangover cure.

It's essentially rice porridge done Japanese style, which means that it's packed with umami from *dashi* and seasoned with the holy trinity of sake, soy sauce, and mirin (a sort of sweet rice wine). Dashi, a stock that forms the foundation of so much Japanese food, is made by steeping kombu (a kind of kelp) and *katsuoboshi* (shavings of smoky preserved bonito fish). Here, though, they suggest using the instant powdered version beloved by chefs the world over. Drizzle in some eggs last minute and let the revivification begin.

Japanese Congee   SERVES 6

1 ounce bonito fish broth powder, preferably Hon Dashi

½ ounce kombu dashi powder

2 cups steamed white rice

¼ cup sake

2 tablespoons mirin

2 tablespoons soy sauce

Kosher salt

2 large eggs, roughly beaten

1 ounce dried wakame seaweed, soaked in water for 5 minutes until softened, then drained

1 bunch scallions, sliced into 1-inch pieces

Grilled salmon or chicken, for serving (optional)

Bring 3½ cups of water to a boil in a medium saucepan. Add the bonito powder and the kombu powder and cook until they dissolve, 1 to 2 minutes. Add the rice, lower the heat to maintain a gentle simmer, and cook uncovered, stirring occassionally, until the rice is incredibly soft and the grains have broken down, about 1 hour.

Stir in the sake, mirin, soy sauce, and salt, then stir in the eggs and cook until just barely set, 30 to 45 seconds. Stir in the wakame and scallions and divide among 6 bowls. Serve with grilled salmon or chicken, if you like.

Le Chateaubriand

PARIS, FRANCE

It's a tale as old as time: A French-Basque boy leaves home, develops a love for cooking in Tel Aviv at an age (twenty-seven) when most wannabe super-chefs are moving onto their eighth chef de cuisine gig, then opens a restaurant that changes Parisian dining. Okay, the truth is, the story of Iñaki Aizpitarte's rise is as about as ordinary as his name is pronounceable. When he opened Le Chateaubriand, a scruffy bistro in the eleventh arrondissement, in 2006, the self-taught chef ushered in a *new* new revolution in French food. First it was the top cooks at the city's grand two– and three–Michelin starred restaurants who struck out on their own, cooking technique-driven food and selling it at prices those same cooks could actually afford. (Food nerds, see: Camdeborde, Yves.) Yet the haute cuisine defector Camdeborde and his Le Comptoir family of restaurants are Paris's rock 'n' roll, then Aizpitarte is pure punk—simplicity over bombast, driven by love for the process.

When he goes out, he's drawn to like-minded cooks but respects the old guard, too. So he and his friends had snacks at Chez Aline (in a former horse butcher shop—hence the name, a playful tweak on *chevaline*), which sells unassuming sandwich triumphs like pot-au-feu on a baguette. They had G&Ts at Clamato (just as Aizpitarte located the even-less-formal Le Dauphin next door to Le Chateaubriand, Bertrand Grébaut's seafood-focused spot is next to impossible-to-get-into Septime). Then they bumped into Alain Ducasse, or as Aizpitarte calls him, "The Pope," an appropriate nickname for a chef who hoards Michelin stars like *Benedict* XVI did flamboyant red shoes.

By the time they'd mowed down headcheese and clams cooked with white wine and butter at Le Verre Volé and too much mezcal at El Cafe Bar ("a very Parisian bar without a Parisian name"), Aizpitarte wasn't capable of executing the dish with which he often ends drunken nights. If it seems tame for a renegade chef, remember: just as you can't make an omelet without cracking eggs, you can't become the talk of Paris without knowing how to make a proper omelet. And by that we don't mean the scorched cylinder of egg filled with spinach and feta that passes as one on our side of the Atlantic. Do it his way, and you've got a pillowy perfection that takes nothing more than good eggs, good butter, and approximately two decades of experience. So instead of sharing a recipe reflective of Aizpitarte's hard-won skill, we thought we'd share a hangover-friendly version, a great omelet made with a few corners cut for cooks undertaking bleary mornings after.

The scorched omelets of late nights and hard mornings here in the States are a French chef's nightmare. Crammed with broccoli and Kraft or spinach and feta, they're the antithesis of the Spartan omelets that tickle those raised on Reblochon and andouillete, and require little more embellishment than a sprinkle of chives. The keys to the creamy, ethereal proper omelet are a non-stick pan, a healthy knob of butter, and practice. Yet even if the latter eludes you, you can still take a big step forward just by using the former and laying off the broccoli.

An Omelet   SERVES 1

3 large eggs

Kosher salt

1 tablespoon unsalted butter

In a small bowl, whisk the eggs and a pinch of salt until well-aerated and the yolks and whites are well combined.

Heat a nonstick skillet over medium-low, add the butter, and swirl to coat the sides of the pan.

Pour the eggs into the skillet and let sit. Once the edges of the omelet begin to rise, after about 2 minutes, take a rubber spatula and gently push the set edges toward the middle of the pan, allowing the uncooked egg to run toward the sides of the pan. Cook for about 45 seconds, then flip the omelet with a spatula and cook the second side for another 45 seconds.

Pick up the pan by the handle, tilting it downward, and use the spatula to fold the edge closest to the handle down to the center. Slowly slide the omelet onto a plate and use the pan to fold the already folded part onto the unfolded section.

Birch and Barley

WASHINGTON, D.C.

Under the nose of D.C.'s culinary giants, young gun Kyle Bailey was quietly making some of D.C.'s most-wanted food by going old school. José Andrés made his name in the capital spherifying clams, and Michel Richard made his composed sashimi mosaics, but Bailey got noticed for making simple, playful food made almost entirely from scratch—from pasta and breads to charcuterie and kraut. Bailey never crosses the line into off-puttingly fancy—this is the guy who won us over with bowls of pasta inspired by a trip to Philly, not Puglia. Why use bread when the elements of the city's other iconic sandwich—roast pork with broccoli rabe—taste so good on ricotta cavatelli?

Even when he gets blotto, he can't shake the homemade-everything aesthetic. So he roped his pastry-pro wife into remaking the humble ham and cheese Hot Pocket, the hangover breakfast we ate before we were old enough to buy lotto tickets, let alone handles of Stoli. And not just any Hot Pocket, but one the size of a toddler who eats too many Hot Pockets. It broke a few of the rules of Hot Pocket cookery in that it requires effort (but only a little) and doesn't require the microwave. Not only that: Bailey cooked it on a Himalayan salt block in a pizza oven. Please don't try that at home.

KYLE BAILEY

1 teaspoon active dry yeast

2 cups warm water (115°F)

2 pounds "00" flour, plus more for dusting

2 tablespoons extra-virgin olive oil

2 tablespoons honey

1 tablespoon kosher salt

¾ pound shredded cheddar cheese (the orange kind, not white)

¾ pound shredded Monterey Jack cheese

1 pound shaved ham

2 large eggs

2 teaspoons milk or water

Giant Ham and Cheese Hot Pocket   MAKES 3 TO SERVE 6 TO 8

In the bowl of a stand mixer fitted with a dough hook, combine the yeast and water. Let sit until foamy, about 10 minutes, then add the flour, olive oil, honey, and salt. Knead on medium speed until a smooth dough forms, about 10 minutes. Cover with a damp towel and let proof in a warm spot until doubled in size, about 1 hour.

Divide the dough into 6 equal-sized balls and transfer to a baking sheet. Cover with a damp towel and allow to proof in a warm spot for another hour.

Heat the oven to 500°F. Line 3 baking sheets with parchment paper. In a bowl, toss together the cheddar and Jack cheeses. On a lightly floured surface, roll out 1 ball of dough to a 12 by 8-inch rectangle and transfer to a prepared baking sheet. Top the dough with one-third (½ pound) of the cheese and one-third (⅓ pound) of the ham, leaving a 1-inch border all around.

Roll out another ball of dough to a 12 by 8-inch rectangle. In a small bowl, beat the eggs with the milk or water and brush the edges of the filling-topped dough. Then, place the second piece of dough on top and, using a fork, crimp the edges to seal them. Brush the top with more egg wash and bake until golden, about 15 minutes. Repeat the process with the remaining dough, cheese, and ham to make two more hot pockets while the first hot pocket is baking. Let cool slightly before eating.

Acme

SYDNEY, AUSTRALIA

Mitch Orr is too young to be this good at making pasta. But the thirty-something chef, who trained at Massimo Bottura's Osteria Francescana in Modena before opening Acme in Sydney, extrudes linguine, rolls strozzapreti, and forms agnolotti like a goddamn nonna. And not just any nonna, but one who grew up in the Australian immigrant city, where some whisper that the Asian food is better than in, you know, Asia. Orr takes his lovingly made pasta and tosses it with black garlic and burnt chile so it's as much a riff on the classic *spaghetti aglio, olio, e peperoncino* as it is on the beloved Malaysian stir fry mee goreng. Housemade macaroni gets a sauce of sisig, the sweet-and-tangy Filipino dish of pig's head simmered until tender, then crisped in a hot skillet. In Sydney, where pasta tends to end up either on white tablecloths or red-checkered ones, Orr is staking out a delicious middle ground.

We rode with him around Sydney, eating Burrata cheese injected with shellfish oil at Automata, where the light fixtures were made from old Ducatti engines; getting meat sweats at LP's Quality Meats, where a smoker shipped in from Tennessee yielded gout-inducing deliciousness like smoked beef tongue with bone marrow vinaigrette; and finally going hard at Cantonese seafood emporium Golden Century, where he and his chef friends once went with their chefs when they were just wee line cooks.

After they ordered live scallops and abalone, the waiter brought them from the fish tanks to the table for inspection before they were cooked. Here is where we learned, as a plate of it hit the table, that Orr's pick for Australia's national dish is salt-and-pepper squid. If this is Orr's fried calamari, it's no wonder his pastas are about as Italian as pad thai. By the time lap dances at Bada Bing were done, and everyone back at Acme was hungry, Orr was making bologna sandwiches with foie gras butter and, in a mysterious turn, blooming onions, which we could've sworn had nothing to do actual Australia and more to do with the American caricature of the country called Outback Steakhouse. As soon as salted caramel–drizzled donut holes came out, the mystery was solved— who cares when there's donuts?

If you've only ever *eaten* donuts, you'll be surprised at how entirely doable they are to make. If you've *made* donuts, you'll be surprised at what potato—yeah, you read that right—can do for them. Adding a little in the dough makes the donut holes fry up to the perfect texture, right in between the fluffiness of yeast donuts and the substantial crumb of the cake variety. Not that it matters all that much when there's salted caramel.

DONUT HOLES

½ pound russet potatoes, peeled and cut into 1-inch pieces

¾ cup plus 1 tablespoon whole milk

½ cup granulated sugar

2¼ teaspoons active dry yeast

1 large egg

1 large egg yolk

3½ cups "00" flour

1½ teaspoons kosher salt

5 tablespoons unsalted butter, melted

2 tablespoons ground cinnamon

Vegetable oil, for frying

SALTED CARAMEL

1½ cups light brown sugar

16 tablespoons (2 sticks) unsalted butter

¾ cup heavy cream

Kosher salt

Cinnamon-Sugar Donut Holes with Salted Caramel   MAKES 2 DOZEN

To make the donut holes, in a medium saucepan, cover the potatoes with water, salt generously, and bring to a boil over high heat. Turn down the heat to maintain a simmer and cook until soft, about 20 minutes. Drain, then mash the potatoes.

In a small saucepan, combine ½ cup plus 1 tablespoon of the mashed potatoes and the milk and warm to 115°F over medium heat. Add ¼ cup of the sugar and the yeast, mix well to combine, then remove from the heat. Let sit until foamy, about 10 minutes.

Transfer the mixture to the bowl of a stand mixer fitted with a paddle attachment and add the egg and yolk. Mix well, then add the flour and salt. Mix on medium speed until a smooth dough forms, about 5 minutes, then let rest for 15 minutes. Stir in the melted butter and cover with plastic wrap. Allow the dough to rise in a warm place until doubled in size, about 1 hour.

Line a baking sheet with parchment paper. Break the dough into 24 equal-sized balls and transfer to the prepared baking sheet. Cover with plastic wrap and allow to rise again in a warm place for another hour.

In a large bowl, mix the remaining ¼ cup of sugar and the cinnamon and set aside.

Heat 4 inches of oil in a large saucepan until a deep-fry thermometer reaches 325°F. Fry the donuts, turning as needed, until golden and cooked through, 4 to 5 minutes. Using a slotted spoon, transfer the donuts to paper towels to drain. Let cool slightly, then toss in the cinnamon-sugar mixture.

To make the caramel, in a heavy-bottomed medium saucepan, cook the brown sugar until it begins to caramelize, about 6 minutes. Add the butter and cream and whisk until smooth and combined. Season to taste with salt. Pour the caramel over the donuts or serve as a dipping sauce.

St. John Bread and Wine

LONDON, ENGLAND

Lee Tiernan came up under the tutelage of Fergus Henderson, the originator of nose-to-tail cooking and the reason every chef on Earth serves an app of roasted marrow bones with toast. Now, Tiernan runs Black Axe Mangal, his ode to London's Turkish barbecue spots, where a wood-burning oven painted with portraits of every member of KISS cranks out killer flatbreads topped with, oh, lamb tongue spiked with Sichuan peppercorns. But before that, for nearly ten years, Tiernan ran the kitchen at the slightly chiller Bread and Wine outpost of Henderson's game-changing London restaurant St. John, overseeing an odd bits-heavy menu of blood cakes and pig's ear. Besides learning to cook from the Obi-Wan of offal, he also credits his time working under Henderson for the fortitude of his own personal liver.

On his episode of *Chef's Night Out*, Tiernan started his evening by sharing a pint with his mentor, then hit the town with two mates: a bearded artist and a cheeky sheep farmer. They grabbed a plastic bag full of beers and hit Tiernan's former South London stomping grounds for Pakistani curries at Lahore Karahi. He pulled an equally quintessential Londoner move with a stop at a proper pub—the frozen-in-time Golden Heart. He was a wee bit tiddly, so he moonwalked (literally) down Brick Lane, past the spot where he and his wife had their first kiss, and to the twenty-four-hour Beigel Bake. Instead of ordering his usual—their signature salt beef with mustard slapped on a bagel—he grabbed a couple dozen plain, untouched and still hot-from-the-oven, and hauled them back to Bread and Wine. There, they were split open and packed with thinly sliced ox heart that had been marinated with ginger, lime, and fish sauce and grilled over fire.

It's got the spirit of the food Tiernan now turns out at Black Axe Mangal. Although the dish would never find its way onto Henderson's menu, we bet Lee Boy's old boss would approve.

LEE TIERNAN

Tiernan calls for the heart of an ox, but as far as we can tell, "ox" in the British parlance is to "cow" like "pissed" is to "plastered." Beef heart it is, then. Anyone skittish about eating this particular animal part should keep in mind that (1) it's a muscle, just like steak, (2) it's way cheaper than steak, and (3) it's super tender and full of the beefy flavor you want. A kind butcher will trim off the ventricals and other inedible bits for you. Perhaps she'd even do you a solid and cut it into thin slices. Of course, you can substitute thinly sliced steak, chicken breast, or your favorite brand of tempeh. But then you can't complain when the sandwich sucks.

1 (1½-pound) beef heart, outer and inner membranes trimmed (ask your butcher to do this for you), sliced into ¼-inch thick strips

2 tablespoons canola oil

1 tablespoon fish sauce

1 tablespoon rice vinegar

8 cloves garlic (6 smashed flat and peeled, 2 minced)

1 (2-inch) piece ginger, peeled and cut into ¼-inch-thick coins

2 limes

1 cup mayonnaise, preferably Hellman's

½ cup Asian hot sauce, such as Sriracha

1½ tablespoons freshly squeezed lemon juice

8 bagels (plain, sesame, everything—whatever tickles your fancy), split horizontally

Gem or iceberg lettuce leaves, for serving

Kosher salt and freshly ground black pepper

Beef Heart Bagel Sandwiches   SERVES 8

Combine the beef heart strips, oil, fish sauce, vinegar, 6 cloves smashed garlic, and the ginger in a large bowl. Cut the limes in half and squeeze their juice over the meat. Throw the squeezed lime halves in the bowl for good measure. Toss everything together, then cover the bowl with plastic wrap and refrigerate for 1 hour or up to 4 hours.

Meanwhile, in a bowl, mix the minced garlic, mayonnaise, hot sauce, and lemon juice until well combined. Cover and refrigerate this spicy garlic mayo while the meat marinates.

Fire up a grill. You want this good and hot for cooking the heart. If you don't have a grill, an oiled griddle will do nicely. Has to be smoking hot, though. Remember to use the exhaust fan to deal with the smoke. When your grill is ready, halve your bagels and grill the cut sides until nicely toasted, 1 to 2 minutes. Spread the bagels with the spicy garlic mayo and set aside on a platter.

Season the heart slices with salt and pepper, then remove each from the bowl and grill until just tender (they should still have the slightest tinge of pink in the center), 20 to 30 seconds per side. As the strips of heart are cooked, place them on the bottom halves of the bagels. Cover with lettuce leaves and the bagel tops. Serve at once with ice-cold American-style beer—lots of it.

Toro

NEW YORK, NEW YORK

Jamie Bissonnette is renowned for a few things—serious hustle, a gifted hand with charcuterie and offal, and, at least since his episode aired, the ability to go H.A.M. His career kicked off when he got kicked out of high school (and his punk band) and found his place in the kitchen. He made his way to Boston, where he became the protégé of Ken Oringer, staging with him at high-end Clio before teaming with his mentor to open Toro and Coppa, the kind of casual, amazing restaurants the city's cooks would go to after their shifts. When the two launched the mammoth outpost of Toro in Chelsea, he moved to Manhattan and went gonzo with a menu dotted with plenty of jamón as well as the deftly tweaked Spanish tapas he's so good at. It's a place to get classics like blood sausage tricked out with apple butter and Basque cheese, or should-be-classics like shaved smoked beef heart on romesco-slathered toast. His food is so him that his antics are easily forgiven.

The escapade began politely when he met up with Oringer and pals for snacks at his New York City happy place: April Bloomfield's John Dory Oyster Bar. He rolled in toting cocktails for the staff, aka boomerangs, so called because they'll come back to you on some future night when the staff shows up at his restaurant. Bissonnette brought boomerangs made with Fernet and Campari, packed in plastic pint containers, and helpfully labeled with "Thanks" and a crude drawing of someone's member. Once he and his friends had freaked out over the quality of the sea creatures there, Bissonnette joked about doing raw clam stuntman shots—snort the horseradish, shoot the bivalve, squeeze the lemon into your eye, and apply the cocktail sauce to your anus. Little did we know, he was foreshadowing.

The rest of the evening was a blur—a sword was unsheathed to open Champagne, wines that smelled like diapers were drunk, more Champers poured from high above mouths—especially after the actual stuntman shots (salt, tequila, lime) commenced. "We're not doing that again," he said as he left the Four-Faced Liar in the West Village. Sure you're not.

At last, he was back at Toro, and in the kitchen, eyeing the miscellaneous mise en place he'd asked his cooks to leave out for inspiration—it was *Animal House* meets *Chopped*. The result was magic: quesadillas with uni and American cheese, halal cart–style fried rice with pork belly, and, even though he didn't remember it the next day, another stuntman. The camera doesn't lie.

Bissonnette knows his way around a hangover. His go-to cure utilizes the mise en place that is your pantry: scrambled eggs, bread, and potato chips doused with hot sauce. The eggs-with-slightly-soggy-crunchy-chip effect is as sneaky-sophisticated as it is in its true *tortilla española* form. As the wise chef advises, it can be served two ways, and your choice will probably depend on whether you can remember the last drink you had: in mayo-slicked sandwich form or constructed inside the bag of chips, a la the Fritos-inspired Walking Tacos.

3 large eggs

1 tablespoon unsalted butter

Kosher salt and freshly ground black pepper

1 (1½-ounce) bag plain potato chips, preferably Lay's Classic

2 slices whole-wheat bread

Hot sauce

Mayonnaise (optional)

Olive oil (only if you can remember the last drink you had)

Scrambled Eggs and Potato Chips SERVES 1

FOR A SUPER BAD HANGOVER: Crack the eggs into a bowl. Beat with a fork until they are all homogeneous.

In a small nonstick skillet, heat the butter over medium. When it starts to coat the bottom, add the eggs and season with salt and pepper. Stir until the eggs start to set, then pull the pan from the heat, open the bag of chips, and crush them in the bag. Dump them into the eggs, and stir until the eggs are set but still runny. Transfer the eggs to the chip bag and let everything sit.

Toast the bread over a flame (or use a toaster). When the bread is toasted, tear it up, put it into the bag, douse the bag's contents with hot sauce to taste, hit the couch, and eat straight outta the bag.

FOR A *NOT* SUPER BAD HANGOVER: Crack the eggs into a bowl. Beat with a fork until they are all homogeneous.

In a small nonstick skillet, heat the butter over medium. When it starts to coat the bottom, add the eggs and season with salt and pepper. Stir until the eggs start to set, then pull the pan from the heat, open the bag of chips, and crush them in the bag. Add them to the eggs and turn up the heat to medium-high. Run a spatula under the eggs to make sure they aren't sticking, then flip the eggs onto a plate. Add some olive oil to the pan, return the eggs to the pan, and cook for 2 to 3 minutes. Flip again and cook for 2 to 3 more minutes, until the eggs are completely set. Transfer back to the plate. Toast the bread in a toaster. Make a sandwich with the hot sauce and mayo and the egg and chip mixture.

Acknowledgments

EDITORS OF MUNCHIES

Thank you to MUNCHIES executive producers Chris Grosso and Lauren Cynamon. We wouldn't exist or be where we are without you. Thanks to the crew that came up with the idea of *MUNCHIES*—the original title for *Chef's Night Out*—and executed our early episodes: Jesse Pearson, Chris Cechin, and Thobey Campion.

Special thanks to Farideh Sadeghin, who helped gather all of the recipes for this book, spearheaded a team of recipe testers, styled photos, and provided us with too many dirty jokes.

Thanks to MUNCHIES Publisher John Martin, who jumpstarted this entire cookbook process and convinced us that print is not analogue. Thank you to Tommy Lucente, who graciously herded all of the cats for us. Thanks to Nyasha Shani Foy and Leslie Stern for their continuous support in our delicious efforts.

Thank you to our friends at FremantleMedia; especially Keith Hindle and Elena Magula, and the Tiny Riot team: Regina Leckel, Devon Dunlap, Jessica Porper and Nathan Rea.

A very special thanks to Mario Batali and Reyna Mastrosimone. *Cin-cin*, motherfuckers!

Thank you so much to our agents at the Gernet Company: David Gernert, Anna Worrall, Chris Parris-Lamb, and Paula Breen for helping to make this dream become reality. Thank you to the entire staff at Ten Speed and Crown, and especially Maya Mavjee, Aaron Wehner, Hannah Rahill, Windy Dorresteyn, Serena Sigona, David Hawk, Daniel Wikey, and Allison Renzulli.

A massive thanks to our amazing cookbook editor, Emily Timberlake, who wrestled with our Cheetos-encrusted dreams and turned them into a printed expression of who we are. Thanks to Kara Plikaitis for making this thing look beautiful, despite our dumpster-diving aesthetic tendencies.

Thanks to Brayden Olson and Justin Hager for being willing to get creative and weird with the images in this cookbook.

Thank you to our Southern recipe wrangler and tester Ben Mims. All we can say is "SAME." A big thanks to Yewande Komolafe and Alex Laudeman for their relentless help and knowledge in the test kitchen during the photo shoot. Rupa Bhattacharya, thank you for being our secret weapon throughout this project. Big love and thanks to our incredible kitchen interns: Jacqueline Ventura, Elizabeth Williams, Alex Burris, and Rodney Farquhar for helping us during this cookbook process. You are also beautiful hand models.

248

Thanks to Barry Frish, our kitchen manager, for ordering all of the ingredients, including the extra pig's head that's still in the freezer.

Thank you to Nathan Mell and the entire team at Felt + Fat for providing your beautiful pottery to put these glorious late-night fever dream dishes on something beautiful.

Thanks to our incredible props stylist, Rebecca Bartoshesky, who saved the day and magically sourced bizarre objects from thin air as if she were David Blaine (back when he was at his prime in the late '90s).

Additional thanks to Gayle Gilman, Erica Winograd, Tracy Wares, Patrick Maguire, Shawn Phelan, Lee Tiernan, Lars Hinnerskov Eriksen, Bernardo Loyola, Khoung Phan, James Quinn, Elana Schulman, Peter Courtien, Bernardo Garcia, Randy Foreman, Peter Spark, Justin Cymbol, Brad Barrett, Zoe Kanan, Cal Elliott, Francesco Grosso, Olivia Young, Action Bronson, and Danny Minch.

Thanks to VICE co-founders Shane Smith and Suroosh Alvi, co-presidents Andrew Creighton and James Schwab, and the entire VICE team.

A massive thanks and gratitude to the entire MUNCHIES family around the globe: let's continue to operate this strangely beautiful all-you-can-eat buffet.

And last but not least, thank you to all of the chefs of the past, present, and future who have generously welcomed us into your environments and allowed us to film your drunken adventures. You continue to remind us of why the restaurant industry will never become boring. We're not sorry for the hangovers.

Index

A

Acme, 236, 239
Agg, Jen, 106, 108
Agua Fresca, Cantaloupe, 10
Aikawa, Shion, 59
Aikawa, Tatsu, 59
aioli
    Espresso Aioli, 43
    Lemon Aioli, 51
Aizpitarte, Iñaki, 228, 231
Amass, 76, 78
An American Place, 156
Amis, 32, 35
Anderson, Erik, 6, 28, 30
Anderson, Sam, 6–7
Andrés, José, 44, 232
aquavit
    Midnight Sun, 9
Arakataka, 178
Atelier Crenn, 24, 27
Au Pied de Cochon, 52
Automata, 236
The Avenue Pub, 40
Avila, Wes, 72, 74
avocados
    Guacachile, 87
    Guacamole, 78
    Seven-Layer Dip, 90

B

Baca, Joaquin, 132, 134
bacon
    Bacon-and-Gravy Mac and
        Cheese, 134
    Bacon Tamarind Caramel, 145
    Fried Shrimp and Bacon Grilled
        Cheese, 22
    Late-Night Carbonara, 131

Nasi Lemak, 145
    Stuffed Jacket Potatoes, 98
Badmaash, 100, 105
Bagel Sandwiches, Beef Heart, 242
Bailey, Kyle, 232, 234
Le Bal Café, 216, 219
Bang, Esben Holmboe, 9, 18, 178, 181
Bar Agricole, 60
Barbuto, 156
Bar Isabel, 164, 166
Bar Raval, 166
beans
    Seven-Layer Dip, 90
beef
    Beef Heart Bagel Sandwiches, 242
    Carne Asada Burritos, 78
    Côte de Boeuf, 198
    Meatballs and Red Sauce, 195
    Oxtail Curry with Roti, 183–84
    Seven-Layer Dip, 90
    Taco Beef, 90
    Tongue Chili Nachos, 108
    Tongue Sandwich, 38
    Tripe Sandwiches, 49, 51
beer
    Beer and Butter–Spiked Crab in
        Black Bean Sauce, 169
    Blackout Stout Cake, 209–10
    Carne Asada Burritos, 78
    Fernet Gingerbread with Foie
        Gras Torchon, 214
Beigel Bake, 240
Benno, Jonathan, 48–49, 51
Benu, 146
Bernamoff, Noah, 100, 101
Best Pizza, 110–11
Birch and Bailey, 232, 234
Bissonnette, Jamie, 45, 244, 247

Bitter Margarita, 11
Bitters, Terrarium, 7
Black Axe Mangal, 240
black cod
    Fried Fish Sandwich, 62
Black Hoof, 106, 108
Blackout Stout Cake, 209–10
Blanc, Raymond, 12
Blanca, 190
Bloomfield, April, 54, 56, 244
Bohr, Robert, 152, 155
Bologna, Smoked, and Raclette
        Sandwich, 30
Bombshell, 100, 104
Bones, 216
Bottura, Massimo, 236
Boulud, Daniel, 80
bourbon
    René Angélil, 14
Bourdain, Anthony, 196, 198
Bowien, Danny, 60, 80, 88, 170–72
Brasserie Les Halles, 196
bread
    Chopped Liver on Toast, 56
    Roti, 184
    See also sandwiches
Briones, Mikey, 132
Brioza, Stuart, 182–84
broccoli
    Stuffed Jacket Potatoes, 98
broccolini
    Sautéed Vegetables, Bulgur, and
        Dandelion Salsa Verde, 148
Brock, Sean, 28
Brooklyn Star, 132, 134
Bror, 76
Bulgur, Sautéed Vegetables,
        Dandelion Salsa Verde and, 148

Buns, Pork, 45–46
Burritos, Carne Asada, 78
Butler, Win, 106

C

cabbage
  Fried Fish Sandwich, 62
  Salted Ribs with Braised
    Cabbage, 181
  Sautéed Vegetables, Bulgur, and
    Dandelion Salsa Verde, 148
  Soft-Shell Crab Sliders, 59
El Cafe Bar, 228
Café Boulud, 44
Cajun Coquito, 17
Cake, Blackout Stout, 209–10
Cala, 36
Cámara, Gabriela, 36, 38
Camdeborde, Yves, 228
Campari
  Bitter Margarita, 11
cantaloupe
  Cantaloupe Agua Fresca, 10
  Cantaloupe Juice, 10
Cardamom Rice Pudding, 206
Carmellini, Andrew, 44
Carne Asada Burritos, 78
Casella, Cesare, 196
Castronovo, Frank, 195
Catbird Seat, 28, 30
caviar, 52
Ceviche, Miami-Style, 175
Chan, Sue, 44
Chang, David, 44–46, 80, 110, 132, 186
Charlie Bird, 152, 155, 164
Chassagne, Régine, 106
Le Chateaubriand, 122, 228, 231
cheese
  Bacon-and-Gravy Mac and
    Cheese, 134
  Cheese Quesadillas, 69
  Cheese Sauce, 134
  Chicken Tikka Poutine, 105
  Classic Poutine, 101
  Deep-Fried Camembert, 94
  Dirty Al Pastor Tacos with
    Guacachile, 87
  Fried Shrimp and Bacon Grilled
    Cheese, 22
  Giant Ham and Cheese Hot
    Pocket, 234
  Goat Poutine with Redeye
    Gravy, 104
  Grilled Cheese, 27
  Late-Night Carbonara, 131
  Mortadella Torpedo, 35
  Raclette Cheese Sauce, 30
  Seven-Layer Dip, 90

Shrimp Saganaki with Feta and
  Tomatoes, 176
Smoked Bologna and Raclette
  Sandwich, 30
Stuffed Jacket Potatoes, 98
Tongue Chili Nachos, 108
Tongue Sandwich, 38
Chernow, Michael, 202, 205
Chez Aline, 228
Chez Ammad, 216
Chiang, Han, 32, 160, 163
chicken
  Chicken Tikka Poutine, 105
  Chopped Liver on Toast, 56
  Fried Chicken Fried Rice, 137
  Gemelli Pasta with Peas,
    Chicken, and Mushrooms, 129
  Japanese Congee, 226
  One-Pot Sticky Chicken Wings, 158
  Spicy Chicken Wings, 163
  Tuscan Fried Chicken, 155
Chinese Drunken Noodles, 124
chocolate
  Blackout Stout Cake, 209–10
  Chocolate Chip and Mint Ice
    Cream Sandwiches, 205
  Salted Dark Chocolate
    Pudding, 210
Chocolate Chip and Mint Ice Cream
  Sandwiches, 205
Choi, Roy, 146
Cikowski, Christine, 137
cinnamon
  Cinnamon-Sugar Donut Holes
    with Salted Caramel, 239
  Cinnamon Syrup, 9
Clamato, 228
Classic Poutine, 101
Clio, 244
Coconut–Lemon Curd Tart,
  Toasted, 219
coffee
  Espresso Aioli, 43
  Redeye Gravy, 104
Cohen, Leah, 118, 121
Coi, 146, 148
Cointreau
  Bitter Margarita, 11
Compère Lapin, 17
Le Comptoir, 228
Compton, Nina, 17
Congee, Japanese, 226
Contra, 122, 124
Contramar, 36, 38
Cookies, Chocolate Chip, 205
Coppa, 244
coquito
  Cajun Coquito, 17
  Coquito Mix, 17

Cosme, 190
Côte de Boeuf, 198
crab
  Beer and Butter–Spiked Crab in
    Black Bean Sauce, 169
  butchering, 172
  Butter-Basted Crab Legs with
    Garlic, Ginger, and Chili, 166
  Salt-and-Pepper Crab with Mapo
    Tofu, 171–72
  Soft-Shell Crab Sliders, 59
Crenn, Dominique, 24, 27
Cru, 152
Cucumbers, Quick-Pickled, 45
Cumulus Inc., 94
Curry, Oxtail, with Roti, 183–84

D

Dandelion Salsa Verde, 148
Le Dauphin, 228
Death & Co, 9
De La Torre, Armando, Sr. and Jr., 70
Delmonico, 40
desserts
  Blackout Stout Cake, 209–10
  Cardamom Rice Pudding, 206
  Chocolate Chip and Mint Ice
    Cream Sandwiches, 205
  Fernet Gingerbread with Foie
    Gras Torchon, 214
  Toasted Coconut–Lemon Curd
    Tart, 219
Dip, Seven-Layer, 90
Dirty Al Pastor Tacos with
  Guacachile, 87
Distinguished Wakamba Lounge, 196
DIY Fernet, 7
Donut Holes, Cinnamon-Sugar,
  with Salted Caramel, 239
drinks
  Bitter Margarita, 11
  Cajun Coquito, 17
  Cantaloupe Agua Fresca, 10
  DIY Fernet, 7
  Midnight Sun, 9
  René Angélil, 14
Ducasse, Alain, 228
Dufour, Hugue, 52
Dufresne, Wylie, 126, 129

E

eggs
  Goat Poutine with Redeye
    Gravy, 104
  Late-Night Carbonara, 131
  Nasi Lemak, 145
  An Omelet, 231

eggs, *continued*
   Sautéed Vegetables, Bulgur, and
     Dandelion Salsa Verde, 148
   Scrambled Eggs and Potato
     Chips, 247
   Scrambled Eggs with Uni, 225
Erickson, Maya, 212, 214
espresso. *See* coffee

F
Falcinelli, Frank, 195
Falkner, Elizabeth, 212
Fäviken, 122
fernet, 6, 28
   DIY Fernet, 7
   Fernet Gingerbread with Foie
     Gras Torchon, 214
Filippou, Konstantin, 176
Filipovic, Vanya, 14
fish
   Fried Fish Sandwich, 62
   Japanese Congee, 226
Foie Gras Torchon, Fernet
   Gingerbread with, 214
Forgione, Marc, 156
Four-Faced Liar, 244
Four Horsemen, 122
Frankies 457 Spuntino, 195
Franny's, 142
The French Laundry, 156

G
Garcia, Carlos Llaguno, 196
Gil, Josh, 222, 225
Gingerbread, Fernet, with Foie
   Gras Torchon, 214
Goat Poutine with Redeye Gravy, 104
Golden Century, 236
Golden Heart, 240
Gourmet & More, 24, 27
Grébaut, Bertrand, 228
Grosso, Chris, 32
Guacachile, 87
Guacamole, 78
Guerrilla Tacos, 72, 74
Guisados, 70
Gullo, Abigail, 17
Guu Izakaya, 226

H
halibut
   Fried Fish Sandwich, 62
ham
   Fried Chicken Fried Rice, 137
   Giant Ham and Cheese Hot
     Pocket, 234
Han Dynasty, 32, 160, 163
Hardy, Ryan, 152

Harefield Road, 132
Hemingway, Ernest, 17
Henderson, Fergus, 240
Henry, James, 216
Hija de Sánchez, 84, 87
Ho, Tien, 186, 189
Hollywood Fried Chicken, 80
Holzman, Daniel, 202, 205
Honey Butter Fried Chicken, 137
Hopgood, Geoff, 164
Hopgood's Foodliner, 164
Hot Pocket, Giant Ham and
   Cheese, 234
Husk, 28

I
Ice Cream, Mint, and Chocolate
   Chip Sandwiches, 205

J
Japanese Congee, 226
Jew, Brandon, 60, 62
Joe Beef, 14
John Dory Oyster Bar, 244

K
Kadeau, 96, 98
Kamishima, Shogo, 138, 140
Kelce, Jason, 160
Keller, Thomas, 48, 80, 156
Kemuri Tatsu-ya, 59
Khe-Yo, 169
Kim, Nick, 48
Kofoed, Magnus Høeg, 96
Kofoed, Rasmus, 96
Koslow, Jessica, 10
Krajeck, Philip, 28
Krasinski, Nicole, 182–84
Kulaga, Agatha, 208–10
Kulp, Joshua, 137
Kushima, Taiji, 138, 140

L
Lagasse, Emeril, 40
Lahore Karahi, 240
lamb
   Lamb Tacos with Árbol Chile
     and Pine Nut Salsa, 74
   Salted Ribs with Braised
     Cabbage, 181
Late-Night Carbonara, 131
Lau, Jimmy, 48
Lazy Bear, 212, 214
Lee, Corey, 146
Lemongrass and Thai Basil
   Pork Pie, 189
lemons
   Lemon Aioli, 51

Toasted Coconut–Lemon Curd
   Tart, 219
Lincoln Ristorante, 48–49, 51
Liver, Chopped, on Toast, 56
lobster
   Miami-Style Ceviche, 175
LocoL, 146
LP's Quality Meats, 236
Lung Shan, 170

M
Maaemo, 9, 178, 181
Mac and Cheese, Bacon-and-
   Gravy, 134
Mahendro, Arjun and Nakul, 100, 105
Manfreds, 76
Manzke, Walter, 72
Mapo Tofu, Salt-and-Pepper Crab
   with, 171–72
Margarita, Bitter, 11
Mariscos Jalisco, 10
Martinez, Christina, 160
Mary Celeste, 216
Matheson, Matty, 164
Matsumoto, Tako, 59
Maurseth, Anne, 9
McAndrews, Peter, 32
McConnell, Andrew, 94
McGlone, Morgan, 28
McMillan, David, 14
Mean Sandwich, 80–82
Meatballs and Red Sauce, 195
The Meatball Shop, 202, 205
Meehan, Peter, 44
Meretoro, 36
Mexikosher, 72
mezcal, 18–19
Miami-Style Ceviche, 175
Michael's Genuine Food and
   Drink, 175
Midnight Sun, 9
Mile End Deli, 100, 101
Miller, Brian, 9
Mina, Michael, 206
Minch, Danny, 11
Mirarchi, Carlo, 18, 190, 192
Mission Chinese Food, 6, 60, 80, 88,
   170–72, 190
Mister Jiu's, 60, 62
Momofuku, 44–46, 132, 186
   Milk Bar, 88, 90
   Noodle Bar, 80, 132
Morin, Fréd, 14
Mortadella Torpedo, 35
Motorino, 195
Murphy, James, 122

mushrooms
  Gemelli Pasta with Peas,
    Chicken, and Mushrooms, 129
  Salt-and-Pepper Crab with Mapo
    Tofu, 171–72
mutton
  Salted Ribs with Braised
    Cabbage, 181
M. Wells Dinette, 52
My Two Cents, 22

N
Nachos, Tongue Chili, 108
Nasi Lemak, 145
Neta, 48
Noma, 76, 84, 122
noodles. *See* pasta and noodles
Nørregaard, Nicolai, 96, 98
No. 16, 178
Nutter, Samuel, 76

O
Obraitis, Sarah, 52
Ogasawara, Masaru, 226
Olvera, Enrique, 18–19, 36, 66, 69
An Omelet, 231
One-Pot Sticky Chicken Wings, 158
Onions, Pickled, 51
Oringer, Ken, 244
Orlando, Matt, 76, 78
Orr, Mitch, 236, 239
Osteria Francescana, 236
Osteria Morin, 131
Ovenly, 208–10
Oxtail Curry with Roti, 183–84

P
Pad Thai, 121
Paesano's, 32
Palcu-Chang, Haan, 216
Parr, Rajat, 206
Pasquale Jones, 152
pasta and noodles
  Bacon-and-Gravy Mac and
    Cheese, 134
  Chinese Drunken Noodles, 124
  Gemelli Pasta with Peas,
    Chicken, and Mushrooms, 129
  Late-Night Carbonara, 131
  Pad Thai, 121
Patinkin, Erin, 208–10
Patterson, Daniel, 146, 148
Pearl's Social & Billy Club, 142
peas
  Fried Chicken Fried Rice, 137
  Gemelli Pasta with Peas,
    Chicken, and Mushrooms, 129
Pegu Club, 9
Peking Duck House, 132

Pemoulie, Alex, 80
Pemoulie, Kevin, 80–82
Picard, Martin, 52
pickles
  Pickled Onions, 51
  Pickled Ramps, 137
  Pickled Scallions, 81–82
  Quick-Pickled Cucumbers, 45
  Squash Pickles, 43
Pie, Lemongrass and Thai Basil
    Pork, 189
Pigalle, 9
Pig and Khao, 118, 121
Pinello, Frank, 110–11
Pizza, 110–13, 115
Porchetta, 192
pork
  Breaded Pork Chop Sandwich, 41
  Chinese Drunken Noodles, 124
  Dirty Al Pastor Tacos with
    Guacachile, 87
  Lemongrass and Thai Basil Pork
    Pie, 189
  Porchetta, 192
  Pork Buns, 45–46
  Pulled Pork Tacos, 70
  Sake and Soy–Marinated Pork
    over Rice, 140
  Salted Ribs with Braised
    Cabbage, 181
  Shrimp and Chili Paste Pork Loin
    Tacos, 81
  See also bacon; ham; sausage
Potato Chips, Scrambled Eggs
    and, 247
potatoes
  Chicken Tikka Poutine, 105
  Classic Poutine, 101
  Goat Poutine with Redeye
    Gravy, 104
  Stuffed Jacket Potatoes, 98
poutine, 100
  Chicken Tikka Poutine, 105
  Classic Poutine, 101
  Goat Poutine with Redeye
    Gravy, 104
Prime Stache, 160
The Progress, 182
puddings
  Cardamom Rice Pudding, 206
  Salted Dark Chocolate
    Pudding, 210
Puglisi, Christian, 76
Pujol, 36, 66, 69
Pulled Pork Tacos, 70

Q
Quesadillas, Cheese, 69
Quillet, Alice, 216, 219

R
Raclette Cheese Sauce, 30
Ragout, 12
Rakel, 156
Ramen Tatsu-ya, 59
Ramps, Pickled, 137
Redeye Gravy, 104
Redzepi, René, 84
René Angélil, 14
Republique, 72
Restaurant Konstantin Filippou, 176
Reynolds, Alisa, 22
Ribs, Salted, with Braised
    Cabbage, 181
rice
  Cardamom Rice Pudding, 206
  Fried Chicken Fried Rice, 137
  Japanese Congee, 226
  Nasi Lemak, 145
  Sake and Soy–Marinated Pork
    over Rice, 140
Richard, Michel, 232
River Café, 54
Roberta's, 190, 192, 195
Rolf and Daughters, 28
Roti, 184
Rubicon, 182
rum
  Cajun Coquito, 17
  DIY Fernet, 7

S
St. John Bread and Wine, 240, 242
Sake and Soy–Marinated Pork over
    Rice, 140
salmon
  Japanese Congee, 226
salsas. *See* sauces and salsas
Salumeria Rosi, 196
Sánchez, Rosio, 18, 84, 87
Sandhi Wines, 206
sandwiches
  Beef Heart Bagel Sandwiches, 242
  Breaded Pork Chop Sandwich, 41
  Chocolate Chip and Mint Ice
    Cream Sandwiches, 205
  Fried Fish Sandwich, 62
  Fried Shrimp and Bacon Grilled
    Cheese, 22
  Grilled Cheese, 27
  Mortadella Torpedo, 35
  Scrambled Eggs and Potato
    Chips, 247
  Smoked Bologna and Raclette
    Sandwich, 30

sandwiches, *continued*
   Soft-Shell Crab Sliders, 59
   Tongue Sandwich, 38
   Tripe Sandwiches, 49, 51
sauces and salsas
   Cheese Sauce, 134
   Dandelion Salsa Verde, 148
   Raclette Cheese Sauce, 30
   Red Sauce, 195
   Salsa, 74
   Salsa Fresca, 78
   Seaweed Tartar Sauce, 62
sausage
   Mortadella Torpedo, 35
   Smoked Bologna and Raclette
     Sandwich, 30
   Tongue Sandwich, 38
Scallions, Pickled, 81–82
Schwader, Phet, 169
Schwartz, Michael, 175
sea urchins, 225
   Scrambled Eggs with Uni, 225
seaweed
   Japanese Congee, 226
   Seaweed Tartar Sauce, 62
Septime, 228
Seven-Layer Dip, 90
Shangri-La, 59
shrimp
   Fried Shrimp and Bacon Grilled
     Cheese, 22
   Pad Thai, 121
   Shrimp and Chili Paste Pork
     Loin Tacos, 81
   Shrimp Saganaki with Feta and
     Tomatoes, 176
Shuko, 48
Simmons, Gail, 142
Snukal, Daniel, 222
Soft-Shell Crab Sliders, 59
Speer, Callie, 100, 104
Spence, Brad, 32, 35, 160
The Spotted Pig, 54, 56
Sqirl, 10
Squash Pickles, 43
Sripraphai, 131
State Bird Provisions, 182–84
Stone, Jeremiah, 122, 124

Sukiyabashi Jiro, 10
Supernormal, 94
Suzume, 132
Syrup, Cinnamon, 9

T
Taco Beef, 90
tacos
   Dirty Al Pastor Tacos with
     Guacachile, 87
   Lamb Tacos with Árbol Chile
     and Pine Nut Salsa, 74
   Pulled Pork Tacos, 70
   Shrimp and Chili Paste Pork
     Loin Tacos, 81
Tacos Punta Cabras, 222, 225
Talde, 142, 145
Talde, Dale, 142, 145
Tanabe, Katsuji, 72
Tart, Toasted Coconut–Lemon
   Curd, 219
Tartar Sauce, Seaweed, 62
Ten Bells, 190
El Tepeyac, 70
tequila, 18
   Bitter Margarita, 11
   Cantaloupe Agua Fresca, 10
Terrarium Bitters, 7
Thirty Acres, 80
Tiernan, Lee, 240, 242
tofu
   Pad Thai, 121
   Salt-and-Pepper Crab with
     Mapo Tofu, 171–72
tomatillos
   Salsa, 74
tomatoes
   Goat Poutine with Redeye
     Gravy, 104
   Meatballs and Red Sauce, 195
   Oxtail Curry with Roti, 183–84
   Pizza, 110–13, 115
   Salsa Fresca, 78
   Seven-Layer Dip, 90
   Shrimp Saganaki with Feta and
     Tomatoes, 176
Tonga Hut, 72
tongue

Tongue Chili Nachos, 108
Tongue Sandwich, 38
Toro, 244, 247
tortilla chips
   Tongue Chili Nachos, 108
tortillas
   Carne Asada Burritos, 78
   Cheese Quesadillas, 69
   Dirty Al Pastor Tacos with
     Guacachile, 87
   Lamb Tacos with Árbol Chile
     and Pine Nut Salsa, 74
   Pulled Pork Tacos, 70
   Scrambled Eggs with Uni, 225
   Shrimp and Chili Paste Pork
     Loin Tacos, 81
Tosi, Christina, 88, 90
Toups, Isaac, 40–41, 43, 45
Toups' Meatery, 40–41, 43
Trattles, Anna, 216, 219
Tripe Sandwiches, 49, 51
Tuscan Fried Chicken, 155

U
Uni, Scrambled Eggs with, 225

V
Valvo, Frank, 94
van Gameren, Grant, 164, 166
Le Verre Volé, 228
Vetri, Marc, 32
vodka, 12
von Hauske, Fabian, 122, 124

W
Wagman, Victor, 76
Walter Foods, 11
Waxman, Jonathan, 156
wd-50, 126, 129
White, Michael, 48, 131
Wildair, 122
W.P. Gold Burger, 138, 140

Z
Zagar, Isaiah, 160
Zimin, Alexei, 12
Zimmern, Andrew, 156, 158

A QUICK GUIDE TO CUP EQUIVALENTS FOR LIQUID

US cups	Metric equivalent	Imperial equivalent
¼ cup	60ml	2fl ox
½ cup	120ml	4fl oz
¾ cup	180ml	6fl oz
1 cup	240ml	8fl oz

First published in the United States in 2017 by Ten Speed Press, an imprint of the Crown
Publishing Group, a division of Penguin Random House LLC, New York.

This edition is published by arrangement with Ten Speed Press, an imprint of the Crown
Publishing Group, a division of Penguin Random House LLC, New York.

This edition published in the UK in 2017 by Sphere

10 9 8 7 6 5 4 3 2 1

Grateful acknowledgment is made to the following for permission to reprint
previously published material:

Bloomsbury Publishing Plc: "Côte de Boeuf" from *Les Halles Cookbook* by
Anthony Bourdain, copyright © 2004 by Anthony Bourdain. Reprinted by
permission of Bloomsbury Publishing Plc.

Clarkson Potter/Publishers, an imprint of the Crown Publishing Group, a division
of Penguin Random House LLC: "Pork Buns" from *Momofuku* by David Chang
and Peter Meehan, copyright © 2009 by David Chang. Reprinted by permission of
Bloomsbury Publishing PLC.

HarperCollins Publishers: "Chopped Chicken Liver on Toast" from *A Girl and
Her Pig* by April Bloomfield, copyright © 2012 by April Bloomfield. Reprinted by
permission of Canongate.

HarperCollins Publishers: "Salt-and-Pepper-Crab with Mapo Tofu" from *The
Mission Chinese Food Cookbook* by Danny Bowien and Chris Ying, copyright ©
2015 by Danny Bowien and Chris Ying. Reprinted by permission of HarperCollins
Publishers.

Workman Publishing Co., Inc.: "Tomato Sauce" and "Spuntino Way," adapted from
The Frankies Spuntino Kitchen Companion & Cooking Manual by Frank Falcinelli,
Frank Castronovo, and Peter Meehan, copyright © 2010 by Frank Falcinelli, Frank
Castronovo, and Peter Meehan. Reprinted by permission of Workman Publishing
Co., Inc., New York. All rights reserved.

A CIP catalogue record for this book is available from the British Library.

ISBN: 978-0-7515-7178-3

Design by Kara Plikaitis

Printed in Italy
Papers used by Sphere are from well-managed forests and other responsible sources.

Sphere
An imprint of
Little, Brown Book Group
Carmelite House
50 Victoria Embankment
London EC4Y 0DZ

An Hachette UK Company
www.hachette.co.uk

www.littlebrown.co.uk